T0231726

The CIO's Guide to Information Security Incident Management

The CIO's Guide to Information Security Incident Management

Eur Ing Matthew W. A. Pemble

CEng FBCS CITP, MIET, CISSP,
Technical Director, Goucher Consulting

Wendy F. Goucher

MBCS Information Security Behaviourism
Specialist, Goucher Consulting

CRC Press
Taylor & Francis Group
Boca Raton London New York

CRC Press is an imprint of the
Taylor & Francis Group, an **informa** business

AN AUERBACH BOOK

CRC Press
Taylor & Francis Group
6000 Broken Sound Parkway NW, Suite 300
Boca Raton, FL 33487-2742

© 2019 by Taylor & Francis Group, LLC
CRC Press is an imprint of Taylor & Francis Group, an Informa business

No claim to original U.S. Government works

Printed on acid-free paper

International Standard Book Number-13: 978-1-4665-5825-0 (Hardback)

This book contains information obtained from authentic and highly regarded sources. Reasonable efforts have been made to publish reliable data and information, but the author and publisher cannot assume responsibility for the validity of all materials or the consequences of their use. The authors and publishers have attempted to trace the copyright holders of all material reproduced in this publication and apologize to copyright holders if permission to publish in this form has not been obtained. If any copyright material has not been acknowledged, please write and let us know so we may rectify in any future reprint.

Except as permitted under U.S. Copyright Law, no part of this book may be reprinted, reproduced, transmitted, or utilized in any form by any electronic, mechanical, or other means, now known or hereafter invented, including photocopying, microfilming, and recording, or in any information storage or retrieval system, without written permission from the publishers.

For permission to photocopy or use material electronically from this work, please access www.copyright.com (http://www.copyright.com/) or contact the Copyright Clearance Center, Inc. (CCC), 222 Rosewood Drive, Danvers, MA 01923, 978-750-8400. CCC is a not-for-profit organization that provides licenses and registration for a variety of users. For organizations that have been granted a photocopy license by the CCC, a separate system of payment has been arranged.

Trademark Notice: Product or corporate names may be trademarks or registered trademarks, and are used only for identification and explanation without intent to infringe.

Visit the Taylor & Francis Web site at
http://www.taylorandfrancis.com

and the CRC Press Web site at
http://www.crcpress.com

One of the pioneers of security incident management, Dr. E. Eugene "Gene" Schultz, Jr., died suddenly and prematurely in October 2011. A prolific researcher and author, he helped found this area as both an academic and professional specialty. He was enthusiastic, exuberant, and a compelling speaker. He was also a great personal friend for both of us and was the person who encouraged us to take our perspectives of this very important area and create a book.

We would dedicate this book to his memory and to his wife, Cathy, and their daughters, Sarah, Rachael and Leah.

Frontispiece cartoon was created for this book by Jim Barker of jimbarker.net.

Contents

Introduction

When computing goes wrong, it can seriously impact the operations and even the viability of the modern business. Successfully managing security incidents, both accidental and malicious, is increasingly significant for many companies as they begin to depend more and more on their online presence or on Internet communications. The increasing numbers of publicized data breaches, and the legal, regulatory and market penalties enforced on organizations are bringing this previously niche aspect of information security to the focused attention of senior corporate executives.

The genesis of this book was a 36-hour-long incident response teleconference starting one Friday evening and continuing, painfully, through in to Sunday morning. Note – one teleconference, not the entire incident. It destroyed two mobile phones, achieved very little (apart from souring those of us on-call against those working shifts) and demonstrated to us both that responsibility for incident management seemed to be fundamentally uncoupled from any understanding of the aims, requirements or constraints either of the technology involved or the people being abused.

The IT department understood neither the regulatory, nor the business environment and had employed management and information systems that proved wholly dysfunctional in the face of this incident. The sizeable and very capable information security team, called in well after the incident was recognised and after core working hours*, simply did not have the necessary staff resource, business authority or budget available to correct these deficiencies (with the urgency required) nor were they permitted the systems access necessary to cope with the immediate technical problems.

In the aftermath, immediate loss of revenue was estimated in the ten to twenty million Pound Sterling range, with direct costs eventually coming to over £2 million. Long-term revenue losses due to customers switching to alternative providers were not available by the time the incident management team moved onto other things, but were expected to be an order of magnitude greater than the direct losses. Much of this could have been prevented if, early on the Friday evening, the right people had agreed the aims of the response effort, understood the business and technical constraints and knew where the right resources were available.

Since then, the variety and vehemence of incident types has increased significantly. Website hacks and other attacks and malware are still big issues, but they are now often controlled by sophisticated organised crime rather than vandals or activists. Sucks sites are largely a historical curiosity – most complaints now occur on social media sites, which makes them more difficult to deal with. Phishing, intellectual property abuse and passing off are all types of attacks that can occur without any connection to the organization's own computer systems.

This proliferation makes it more difficult for the business or IT professional, especially in a smaller company environment, to make the right decisions with the speed and confidence required in an incident scenario.

Who Are You and What Should You Get out of This Book?

There are a large number of books currently available which deal with aspects of incident response and management – largely they are very technical, covering issues such as "intrusion detection" and "computer forensics" and are aimed at the information security professional. This book will look at the business processes of setting up and running an

---

* And after at least three of the people with the most relevant experience had adjourned to a, thankfully local, pub!

incident response organization and will be aimed at the management professional with a standard level of computer technology skills, or an IT operations manager with no or minimal specific security skills.

The book has been formatted in what might, at first appear a slightly strange order, principally being that first section is basic and contains elements that are repeated in more detail further through the book. This is because we decided that someone new to incident response may not realize that they need a "help book" until they really do. At that point, the pressure of the event is likely to make wading through a book looking for the information needed quickly, might add to stress rather than reduce it. So, the first section is a sort of "In case of emergency, please break the glass" section. After that, the book through the basic things need to be ready the next time, to how to set up, run and continually develop an incident response team.

This is a practical book, full of lessons that we have learned so you don't have to. We hope you find it helpful. Good luck in your endeavors.

Another Introduction or, At Least, Another Way of Looking a Things

Let's not beat around the bush here. Incident response is fun. It can also be really quite frightening. I suppose it depends on your tolerance – roller coasters are fun for the adrenaline thrills they evoke and are very, very safe. Tiger wrestling on the other hand ....

The object of this book is to help you maximise the number of information security issues that fall in to the well-understood analogy of the roller coaster and, well, help you to keep clear of all but the most predatory tigers.

Your IT department is here to help you. The helpdesk are here to help – the name is not ironic. Unless your organization is wholly dysfunctional, an outsider attack can bring out the best in your staff. Your job is to prioritise, motivate and direct the effort these people can provide. If you are unlucky, you may find yourself directly involved, in which case you have the very difficult job of ensuring that somebody else is doing your job while you are doing somebody else's. That does actually make sense but is sufficiently contorted that the point is clear – if you are the incident manager: manage, don't do.

Of course, if for some reason you are the ideal person to be the lead investigator or one of their technical specialists, that's not a real problem. Just make somebody else the incident manager. You should not be doing both jobs.

The difficult thing, if I'm honest, isn't managing the first incident or even the third. It is keeping that initial level of achievement and excitement going week after week whilst nearly all of you still have your main jobs to do and, as ever, the threat environment continues to change.

Authors

Eur Ing Matthew W. A. Pemble CEng FBCS CITP, MIET, CISSP, Technical Director, has less early experience than Wendy with incident management, first coming across it as a real-life experience in the mid-1980s, serving with the Royal Navy's "Armilla Patrol" during the Iran/Iraq war. Since then, he has been involved in nuclear weapon and reactor incident management (all training or exercises, thankfully), run security incidents in the financial, charity, government and retail sectors, set up and managed the incident response team for a major financial organization and provided consultancy and support to customers in the vicious throes of incidents, conducting post-incident reviews and formalizing their incident response frameworks.

Having spoken at conferences on subjects as varied as Incident Management Frameworks, current Criminal Attack methodologies, integration of Incident Metrics with the BASEL Banking Risk frameworks, Sarbanes-Oxley controls, ISO27001 and supporting investigations with digital forensics, he is an acknowledged expert in the area. He also works as an advisor to various tools vendors, committed to providing tools that provide the flexibility and security necessary to assist in the control and resolution of incidents.

Wendy F. Goucher MBCS Information Security Behaviourism Specialist, feels like she has lived all her life as part of the support team to someone working on incident response. As a child, it was her Dad who was a manager, and later a director in the construction industry. In those days, incident response meant late night phone calls and even visits by the police when there were incidents on the local site and they couldn't find his phone number. After a few years off to be a student, she then married into the Navy which, especially when she lived in military housing, was like being a constant incident response support service both to her husband and as part of the wives' community.

Later, when Matthew became an incident manager in a very active environment, Wendy found friends and colleagues sometimes thought she was amazingly tolerant in putting up with the impacts of out of hours on-call work. Actually, she wasn't tolerant, she fizzed and boiled inside like anyone would who was juggling the demands of a young family, a husband developing a high quality IM team and her own life including a career as a lecturer in management, without dropping any of them.

It was partly through sharing the experiences of incident response that Wendy became interested in information security, most especially the relationship between security policies and effective business operations, and the problems that can arise when the two are mismatched. She has been an information security consultant herself for several years now and is also currently completing an MSc (Research) in Computer Science at the University of Glasgow investigating the risks of leakage of visual data from mobile devices. She also very much enjoys having the opportunity to speak at conferences, most commonly for ISACA, but actually for all sorts of interesting people.

Thanks

Many people have contributed to this book, through their successes and their mistakes. They remain, possibly for their own good, largely anonymous. Some of them may recognise their, err, "performances" in our dramatisation.

We would like to thank our Techncial Editors, Eve Edelson and Clive Blake, for their corrections, suggestions and, most especially, for their time and effort.

Disclaimer

Finally, this book has been written for the North American wing of the Taylor and Francis Group and to a US style guide. The authors would like to tender our joint apologies to the letter "U" for its involuntary absence from quite so many words.

1
OH, NO. IT'S ALL GONE HORRIBLY WRONG!

It looked insanely complicated, and this was one of the reasons why the snug plastic cover it fitted into had the words 'DON'T PANIC' printed on it in large friendly letters.

Douglas Adams
The Hitchhikers' Guide to the Galaxy

Information in this chapter:

- Recognizing an information security incident
- Preparing for and controlling the initial incident meeting
- Understanding of the issues created by the incident
- Creating a plan for the first stages of investigation and recovery

Introduction

Something has gone horribly wrong. Or not. You're not sure and it doesn't really matter.

You are about to go in to your first incident meeting. You are either in charge of the meeting or responsible for ensuring that the meeting will actually progress to incident resolution. You are almost certainly unsure of exactly what has happened, what has caused it, what you need to do about it and are even unsure of what you are trying to achieve.

There is a brace of things that you will need to consider before you go in.

Firstly, is this actually an incident? Lots of things go wrong – with information, computers, communications – every day without needing to be handled as an incident.

Secondly, don't worry too much about making the perfect decision. The modern managerial world spends a lot of time thinking about how we can justify, normally to our boss, exactly why the decision we made was clearly the most appropriate one in the circumstances. Forget about that – you are going to have to make decisions based on inadequate amounts of unreliable information. Following on from that, you are also going to have to get used to overtly and unconcernedly changing your mind when more or better information comes up. Be open and honest. It's good for you.*

Lastly, your job is to point people in the right direction and keep them from wandering away from the plan, not to come up with all the ideas for fixing things – particularly if you are non-technical. Make sure you have the right people in the meetings (we'll address that in Chapter 2), and you should get all the help they can give, which ought to be "the help you need." If it isn't, you need to make sure you get it sorted for next time (and that's Chapter 3).

Is It an "Information Security Incident"?

It is a sad fact about the ubiquity of computing that computer malfunctions are also ubiquitous. Just because there is an IT or communications issue, doesn't mean that it is security related or that it has reached the level where it needs to be managed as an incident (see Chapter 5 for more details.)

What should be considered?

- Has there been an actual or potential breach of any of the core security principles?
  - Confidentiality
    - Has somebody seen something they shouldn't?
    - Has data been published to an incorrect location?
    - Has a data storage device gone missing?
  - Integrity
    - Has some data been lost or changed?

---

* Please note that this is not necessarily reliable career advice. YMMV!

- Availability*
  - Is one or more critical business support ICT systems down?
- Non-repudiation†
  - Is a partner or customer claiming that a transaction did not happen or was not properly authorised?
  - Is a supplier or other partner disputing a transaction you have entered into?
  - Are you disputing a transaction with a supplier or partner?
- If there is an issue, is this something that the relevant support team are well used to dealing with (and possibly have a Security approved script for handling the issue)?
- Have you had a complaint or report of a security problem?
- Have you been contacted by the media regarding a security issue?
- Is law enforcement wanting to investigate or retrieve information from your IT systems?

Generally, it is much safer to start off treating things as an incident and wind down once you realise it is an overreaction than to try to catch up once Tech Support have been playing with things for a couple of hours.

The Meeting

First things first: you need to concentrate on getting agreement on:

- Impacts
- Aims
- Authority
- Capabilities
- Constraints

---

* In some organisations, availability incidents will be run under a Service rather than a Security lead. However, you will often want to attend initial meetings and ensure that security is represented whenever there is a malicious or negligent cause probable or suspected, law enforcement is interested or where internal disciplinary action or a civil law suit are likely to be considered.

† Okay, this isn't part of the CIA triad, but if any of the newer concepts are included, this is the one that is most generally accepted.

Then you can work the meeting around to suggesting and deciding on:

- Activities
- Reporting

Finally, you can worry about *record-keeping* and auditability – we will discuss it in detail in Chapter 12.

Basic Meeting Management

At this point, it is quite simple:

- There needs to be a meeting chair. Somebody in control who can keep people on and to the point. If you are not this person, make sure you stay close to them.
- *Time*: This should not be a two-hour meeting with a fixed agenda and programmed coffee and biscuits* half way through. The object is to get out of it as quickly as possible so people can get back to the real work of finding out what is going on. If the answer to a question is not obvious in the meeting, don't allow it to turn in to a discussion point. Make sure that somebody has the action to find out for the next meeting.
- *Records*: Have someone taking official notes – you are going to want to be able to reconstruct the scenario later.† Specifically, note any suggestions for additional people who might help and any actions delegated to people.
- *Blamefests*: Even if it is the company culture, this is not the time and place. Don't allow people to get sidetracked in to "fault," even if it is obvious. Be particularly aware of any tendency to "shoot the messenger." You will quickly run out of honest messengers.

First Steps

Impacts What is going on? What has happened? What may be about to happen? What are people concerned is going to be the impact

---

* Cookies if you are American. "Danish," particularly if you aren't.

† If you are really unlucky, Internal Audit may insist on taking this out of your hands.

on the business? It would be nice to be able to say that you don't need to worry too much about technologies, but most businesses are utterly dependent on IT for running the business process, even if it may not have that much to do with the customer interaction.

So:

- What has happened or is still happening?
- What will this do to the business?
- How did we find out?
- Where can we go for more information?

Aims

There will be one or more desired end-points to this little game, and they may not be the same for everybody and some of them may conflict considerably. Remember that the business is likely to be driving towards "return to normal operations," whether that is a sensible desire or not.

Quite simply:

- What are you trying to achieve at this meeting?
- What would be the ideal resolution of this incident?
- What would be an acceptable resolution?

Of particular importance in this is anything you **must do**, to comply with the law, your regulatory environment, any contractual obligations, or otherwise achieve. Somebody will have put you in charge – it is why you are reading this. What do they want you to do? Find and prosecute the culprit?* Make it all go away quietly? Restore normal business functions as soon as possible?

Authority   Who can order actions to be taken, money to be spent, or services to be suspended? And this is real authority – not "But I'll need to have it approved by my manager in the morning before I can action your request" or "That seems reasonable. I will have to put it before next Thursday's Change Board before I can action it, though."

---

* For some definitions of "prosecute" (often confused in practice with "persecute") this is often a key management aim, regardless of whether there actually is a culprit or not.

These people need to be at, or available to be at, the next meeting if they are not already here.

So:

- Who has authority to order actions to be taken that will impact technology?
- Who has authority to order actions to be taken that will impact the business?
- What spending authority do the members of the incident meeting have and who has the next higher authority?
- Who can request actions from your suppliers? Remember that this does not just include security support such as digital forensics or your anti-virus vendor, but will also include technology suppliers such as ISPs, data centres and software vendors and may include others such as legal advisors, travel* and accommodation or document storage.†
- Who has the authority to involve external parties – particularly law enforcement and regulators?

Capabilities You need to consider what you have available to you in terms of immediate resources and where you can go to get more. Remember that at this point, the lack of accurate information is probably your greatest weakness.

- Who is available to you and what are their skills and knowledge?
  - If they are not at this meeting, how can we get in touch with them and when can they become available?
- What equipment do you have?
  - Where is it?
  - Where do we need it?
  - How can we get it there?
- How can you communicate? (Remember, it's no use relying on email if your network is out.)
- What sources of additional information are there?

---

* Possibly needing to be outside of your usual travel policy restrictions as well.
† Wendy would like to point out that your local coffee and sandwich shops may well see some additional business, too!

Constraints What can you not do? Are there legal, contractual or regulatory restrictions? If people already have ideas on next steps, you also need to consider what the business impacts of these might be.

- Is relevant information held by suppliers or third parties and can you get hold of them?
- Is all the relevant information held online or will you need to access back-ups?
- Are there business restrictions which will limit your flexibility to take certain (or all) affected systems out of service for analysis or repair? Might you impact internal or external Service Level Agreements?
- Are there legal restrictions (on monitoring, say) which might impact your corrective activities?
- Are there legal, regulatory or contractual requirements to report the incident external to your organisation? Depending on your jurisdiction, this can include evidence of money laundering or terrorist activity, various types of sexual material (especially child pornography) and suspected losses of personal data.

Second Steps - Activities

The initial meeting phase may well have generated a reasonable number of actions and, depending on resources, this may well be enough. In that case, you may want to postpone further consideration

However, you also need to consider technical activities. These split in to three key areas:

- Information
- Analysis
- Restoration

Simply, the first two are involved in finding out what went on and why. The last is, quite simply, getting things back to normal. Working from your agreed aims and constraints and your current understand of the business impacts, it should be reasonable to agree the priorities of these actions.*

---

* Depending, of course, on how toxic intra-departmental relations are in your organisation.

Clearly, if you do not yet have sufficient information to understand the impacts, this is going to be high on your list. However, don't allow yourself to get bogged down in details. Getting more information is a very easy technical activity, and if you have enough, you can use that resource to accomplish something more productive.

Analysis is often very difficult work. Trying to trace the source of a competent external hack or the initial infection (Patient Zero) for a malware outbreak are neither easy nor quick.

Set the time for the next meeting and, if possible, ensure that the same people are going to be representing the various areas. At this point, no one is likely to have sufficient records or a clear enough picture of the incident itself to make handing over to another representative easy or sensible.

Do try to avoid taking any investigative actions yourself – you will have enough to deal with in managing the incident.

Third Steps - Reporting

At this early stage, you should be looking to report informally to your management chain and to keep it as simple as possible.

- What have you found?
- What is the current and maximum potential business impact?
- Are there any legal or regulatory implications?
- Do you require additional authority or resources?
- What are your current actions?
- When will the next update be?

2

AND, BREATHE ...

Therefore, no plan of operations extends with any certainty beyond the first contact with the main hostile force.

Helmuth von Moltke (the Elder)
On Strategy

Information in this chapter:

- Goals of incident response
- Ongoing management
- Management, media and customers
- Importance of incident context
- Industry/technical context
- Internal pressure – for example, budget
- Taking an early overview

Introduction

Okay, so you have people away doing stuff. It doesn't matter whether they are looking for information, taking initial actions or collecting material (hopefully, in an evidentially sound manner) for subsequent analysis. They may even be trying to find the latest valid backup. But, whatever they are doing, you have a little bit of breathing room.

Of course, unless, you are taking an active part in the investigations work, which we did suggest was not the ideal thing.

Thinking More Deeply about Goals

Before you start doing things, it is worth taking some time to consider what you should actually be doing.

Broadly speaking, there are three categories of goals in Incident Management:

- Understanding what happened (so you can prevent it from happening again or at least mitigate the risk).
- Restoring systems to normal working order (ideally with a fix that will prevent "it," whatever it was, from happening again).
- Letting people know what happened and what will be done about it.

At this stage of the incident, it is best to approach these in reverse order when considering priorities. Just remember that at this stage you probably have very limited information about what has happened and even less idea about what caused it and why.

What Do I Have to Tell People?

Is there immediately or in the near future, any over-riding requirement to report the incident? If there is, there may be restrictions on what activities you can take before you make the report.

The obvious example here is illegal material. In many jurisdictions you must, and in others it is often sensible to, report this before commencing any investigation activities which might corrupt or obscure evidence. However, there may be contractual restrictions (such as PCI-DSS compliance or supporting government systems or data) that limit your freedom to investigate or that require a suitable qualified independent investigator to act.

It is worth noting that reporting requirements for personal data breaches, such as a 72-hour limit under GDPR, are neither "immediate" nor "the near future," unless you have been called in at an unfortunately very late stage.

How Critical to the Business Is Restoration of Service?

Clearly, operational ICT exists to support the wider goals of the organization – "business as usual" is the desired operating mode. If there is freedom to choose between restoration and investigations, it should generally be a matter for the business or even the executive, not for ICT management, to make that choice. So, if you are not having to wait on a response to your report, it is necessary to consider the priority of restoration versus further investigation.

Now, it is almost axiomatic that unless this is another in a series of incidents (in which case we'd hope you would not be needing this initial section of the book) that business pressure will almost always be for service restoration. Operating customer-facing services away from the normal model can result in significant additional immediate costs and even long-term loss of customers, particularly in a commodity industry. It is therefore essential that, as soon as you can, you can provide the business with suitable advice on which they can make their decisions.

It is best to provide a series of options, together with estimated timeframes for your activities and indicating, where reasonable, what investigations activity each option will allow you to perform.

What, When, Why and How?

Providing that you are in a position to conduct significant further investigation work, you also now need to set the team goals. There are, as the title of this section suggests, a number of different questions you may need or want to ask regarding the incident.

Immediate Concerns

What has happened – or what might possibly happen – is generally the most important question that the business would like you to answer. Luckily, it is often the one that, at least at a non-technical level, is often relatively easy. Exactly what happened at a more granular level is usually harder to determine, but unless you are in a position where legal action is required, often less significant.

Depending on the nature of your incident and whether you need to correlate with third party data, you may be interested in when precisely the incident happened. In many cases, this information is, to some degree, trivially available. Receipt time stamps for malware-laden emails, web-server logs for database hacks, connectivity time-outs for Denial of Service Attacks. However, you do need to consider several potential issues. Firstly, the reliability of log source – if the server itself has been attacked, can you rely on the integrity of the log data? And secondly, the correlation of time-stamps between different logs, particularly if you are relying on data from physically separated sources or dealing with small infrastructures that do not implement time synchronisation.

We will also look later at log content. If your organization is new to incident management, you might not be recording quite the information you really need or, necessarily, keeping it for long enough or in a suitable format.

Things You Might Want to Leave for Later   Why an incident occurred is often the hardest question to get a reasonable, never mind an accurate answer to, unless the cause is simple accident (which is a cause often rejected due to the unfortunately too common organizational imperative to find somebody to blame it all on), you are speculating about any attacker's motives. Many internet attacks are essentially undirected – they are not after your organization, or its computers; specifically, you just happen to be a vulnerable target for their methodology or tool. However, at this initial stage, it is worth keeping in mind that you may have not just a malicious cause, but an active and reactive one.*

Discovering exactly how non-trivial incidents happened is really only practical if a very detailed investigation occurs. Sometimes this is required or otherwise appropriate, but if your priority is service restoration, you are likely to lose much of the low-level information necessary for a complete analysis.

Post-incident review is a vital part of the response to most attacks, and these questions are likely to be best left until then.

Ongoing Management

So, now you have an idea what your goals are, what activities you are likely to want to prioritise and if investigations activities are continuing, what further information you are likely to need.

At this point, you should then be considering the next meeting. Unless your organization is particularly small (or, in a larger organization the Incident Response team available is restricted for some reason) you may wish to split the meeting into technical and

---

* This is a particular problem in the case of insider attacks.

non-technical sections. This will allow you to separate the higher-level management of the incident from the detail of findings and further technical actions.*

Who you need, then, at each meeting will vary with the type of incident, as will the order in which you want to hold the meetings.

To Split or Not to Split the Meeting?

If there are only expected to be a few attendees, you would be wasting your time splitting the meeting. And, especially in the initial phases of any incident, you are reasonably likely to receive information that will radically alter your plans, therefore time is vital.

However, you also need to consider the number of people who you will want to attend the meetings and those who will be able to force themselves upon you. Once a meeting gets beyond eight to ten people, somewhat fewer if you are using video or telephone conferencing, it becomes difficult for the more junior people to get their ideas involved. And, especially if this is different sort of incident that those the attendees have experience of, getting left-field ideas from everybody, especially the staff most experienced with up-to-date technology (who are also likely to be amongst the most junior) is important.

Management Meeting

This meeting is largely going to be focused on business priorities and the wider picture. You will probably want support from one of your investigators (unless you fully understand the technical details) and, if there is a significant impact on IT (for example a denial of service attack or a widespread malware infection), from IT management.

The business should send a representative, ideally one with a significant amount of authority, and you may want to have account managers for any suppliers who are affected or otherwise assisting there as well.

---

* Which should go some way to preventing the waste of time explaining to the non-technical attendees what some of the technical details mean.

Internal legal staff may need to be involved. At this stage, you are unlikely to have external legal representatives available, yet, but having one of your internal lawyers present may help refine those questions that will need to be passed for external advice. Additionally, as most ICT people are not that familiar with the legal process, your lawyer should be able to indicate what of the information not yet available will be most helpful to any external or additional internal advisors.

If this is an internal investigation and is not one where you have an agreed protocol with Human Resources, you will need them available – both from the impacted business and, if you have one, from the team that deals with or advises on disciplinary cases. Also, if the impact of the incident is on one or more members of staff, you will need a representative from the business area.

Where there is a mandatory reporting requirement, or where there has been or is likely to be a significant impact on customers, representation from media/customer relations will be helpful.

Technical Meeting

Actually, if you have a reliable lead investigator and there is no need for difficult (dangerous, courageous, risky – complete your own set of scary adjective) decisions to be made, you may not actually need to attend this. But, at this point, you probably will, although you may want to allow the lead investigator to chair it if they have the appropriate experience.

This will largely be those people attending or identified from your initial meeting who are not actively involved in the management meeting. You will clearly need representation from affected areas of IT, including some management support, as well as any affected suppliers (and, possibly, the account managers for those suppliers from within your organization.)

Management, Colleagues, Media and Customers

As you begin to understand the impacts the incident has had or may be about to have, you will need to pass briefings out of the incident meeting, probably approved at the management meeting.

For internal incidents or where there is likely to be legal or disciplinary involvement, be wary of disclosing information which would prejudice that activity. Noting that, for example, "Full details have been passed to the Production Department or HR team" is usually adequate.

Senior Management

As well as the "we have seen we have a problem and we're looking at it" expectation management you will have engaged in earlier, executive management are likely to require a more formal briefing. Current operational impact on the business is clearly important, as are any legal, regulatory or contractual concerns you have identified. Where you are waiting for specialist advice or for more information to be provided, this should also be highlighted, together with when you would expect this to be available.

Possible scenarios for the incident development with timescales and cost estimates would be ideal, but may need to wait until you have more knowledge of the current situation. Do be wary of briefing speculation in detail – even if you headline it as such. People have a tendency to remember the detail but not its categorisation.

Colleagues

Although people are likely to be intensely interested in a security incident, they need to know how to continue doing their jobs. Noting, as an example, that the main website is down and is likely to be so for 24 hours would be sufficient to allow them to deal with customer enquiries. Of course, in the event of major network disruptions, you will need to consider the best way to disseminate this information.

The Public: Media and Customers

These briefings should be prepared by professionals and should be bland and accurate. Do not be tempted to lie, but do consider dissimulation. A simple statement that "We are aware of the problem and it is currently under investigation" is often sufficient, provided that there is not already considerable information on the issue in the public domain. Do make sure that any briefing is vetted by yourself or a trusted technical member of the response team to ensure that there are no technical inaccuracies.

It is also worth considering whether a "Possible Questions" or "Lines to take" brief should be prepared for the media spokesperson or the customer services representatives to use if they are asked follow-up questions. Obviously, this will only be possible if you have further knowledge of the incident which you are prepared to disclose.

What Next?

At this point, it becomes a matter of "rinse and repeat." Investigations and restoration actions will continue and will need to be monitored, adjusted and reported as your knowledge of the incident improves. The business requirement becomes clearer and you progress to an interim solution.

"The end" of the manic phase of Incident Response may look very different depending on the type of incident. For many, restoration of services to normal will look like the end of the incident and, in fact, this is how it is treated within ITIL and ISO20001.

However, investigations activities may continue – working on backups or on the original affected systems if you have transferred services to alternate devices. Where there is a disciplinary or legal case to be considered, the end point of actively managing that as an incident will often be passing the evidence pack to Human Resources or to Legal for their consideration.

Regardless, you need to make sure that all of your notes, evidence and other documentation are retained, suitably secured, so that they can be considered by the Post-Incident Review.

3

THE FIRST DAY OF THE REST OF YOUR LIFE

The ultimate value of life depends on awareness and the power of contemplation rather than upon mere survival.

Aristotle

Information in this chapter:

- Post-incident analysis – distal and root
- Brushing down the team – getting back to normal
- Unwinding emergency changes
- Assessing costs

Introduction

You should, by this point, have stopped actively managing the incident and you are fairly certain that it is unlikely to recur. You have, hopefully, had some food and some sleep. You may have even had a bit of time to catch up with the day job.

However, there will be a lot of loose ends – some actions still continuing, possibly with Legal or HR, and you also need to make sure that you are better prepared for the next incident of this sort and for the next of any sort.

So, clearly, you need to ensure:

- That the incident is completed properly
- You conduct a post-incident review
- You formalise the arrangements for incident response

The last is the driver for the majority of this book, but let us deal briefly with all three.

Completing Activities

Taking Care of the Team

If you are really lucky, your incident has been done and dusted either within a few working days or only requiring intermittent activity over a longer period. This is, unfortunately, often not the case and you and various members of the response team are likely to have been working significantly over hours and to the wholesale detriment of the day job.

Before you relinquish the Incident Manager hat, it is essential that you ensure their transition back into their normal working environment is managed in a way that reflects the effort they have been putting in.

Established incident response teams will have strategies for coping with this including aspects:

- Time off in lieu
- On-call and overtime payments
- Management who are used to members of staff being seconded for incident work

In a new environment, you are likely to have to fight for any or all of these. Unless your organisation has an established system for extra payments, you are unlikely to achieve these at the moment. So concentrate on ensuring that people get time off to recover – possibly speaking with their managers and giving them a few four-day weeks. And, if your company has a "rewards scheme," employ it judiciously. Perhaps an away-day for all of those involved?

Reverting (or Formalising) Changes

During the response activities, you are likely to have used the emergency aspects of your corporate change management system or possibly used some of your business continuity or disaster recovery controls. Some of these may have been already returned to their pre-incident state.

The rest either need to be returned or, if more convenient, put through the change management process to ensure that documentation is properly updated. Technically, this should be somebody else's problem,* but it is worth your time ensuring that it is

---

* ™Douglas Adams (RIP)

being progressed. In future days, when you have a properly running incident management programme, you want the emergency change people to be on your side, not remembering you as having caused them problems in the past.

Post-Incident Review

PIRs are dealt with more fully in Chapter 23, but at this level of evolution of your nascent incident management team, it is best to have something quick and informal.

Just remember why you might be doing this, as the incident is already closed. The main purpose is to get immediate (or very shortly afterwards) feedback to ensure that any areas where it is clear that there were or are problems with the incident process – resources, tools, training or workflow – are identified and can be passed to the relevant manager to see if they can be addressed.

It is worth considering in order:

- What happened?
- Why did it happen?
- Were we appropriately organised and what can we learn for next time?
- Was there any advice or assistance we needed but couldn't get?
- Did we make any reasonably foreseeable mistakes?

At this point, without a comprehensive evidence collection capability, it is unlikely to be worth your while spending too much time on the causes of the incident. It is much more important to look at the successes and failures of the team's decisions and actions and how they may guide you in developing your management processes and controls.

Formalising the Future

At this point, you should be looking to provide a reasoned briefing to management on the practicality of creating a structured incident response process and team. While they are hopefully dazzled by the way you turned the business away from some rapidly oncoming precipice, you may have additional leverage.

The initial decision that should be considered is whether it is appropriate to continue with an ad hoc scheme or you can implement a formal roster.

Regardless, you will need to identify:

- People who were or may be both useful and available
- Communications
- Limitations (if any) of delegated authority
- Successes and limitations of currently available tools
- Any legal or regulatory restrictions or concerns

4

Introducing Amber Inc. and Jade Ltd.

Knowledge without application is like a book that is never read.

Christopher Crawford
Author

Information in this chapter:

- Introduction
- Meeting the organizations
- Why they are making the step to incident response

Introduction

A book that purports to give practical advice on business processes is making a brave claim, not least because organizations and businesses are not generic. They vary in structural terms and also in terms of culture and even the managerial and personal approach, sometimes so much so that advice given could be seen as irrelevant. You don't have to skip too many pages telling yourself "this doesn't apply to me" before you might wonder why you bought, or borrowed, this book at all!

To ease this problem, we decided that from this section onward, at the end of each chapter, the summary would include a discussion of how the points would apply to two very different organizations called Amber Inc. and Jade Ltd.

In the first instance, it would be natural to pay more careful attention to the organization that bears most resemblance to that in which you predominately operate. But do remember that, if Amber Inc. is your closest example, your contractors and suppliers may well best identify with Jade Ltd., and you would do well to get an insight into their perspective at some point. Likewise, if you are a small organization understanding how larger ones similar to your customers' may be dealing with their issues, looking at the other aspect should be helpful.

In short, we recommend that read about your own "side" first, but then go back later, maybe when the pressure is off a bit and refresh your understanding from the perspective of the other organizational model.

Lastly, we must state at this point that these are models. They are not based on any specific organization. We have used our experience in crafting them, but they are a weave of many rather than a mirror of any.

Amber Inc.

Amber Inc. is a multi-national company that produces a range of products. Their IT department consists of some 100 people with a couple of people dedicated to security with particular focus on Firewall and IDS management.

Amber Inc. has an online sales channel, which comprises a small percentage of their business, although their sales team manages to convert many customers who initially buy that way to accounts customers. Although Amber Inc. takes payment for their products ordered through their website, they have outsourced this function to their bank and therefore do not have specific compliance responsibilities for PCI-DSS. Additionally, about 40% of accounts-based customer business is conducted via an online portal and a further significant amount via email.

Amber Inc. has found that over the last 18 months there is increasing pressure from their corporate customers for ISO27001 compliance. As a result, the initial review of existing systems and processes it was decided that it this was the appropriate time to establish an ISMS, including an incident response team.

It has been the board of Amber Inc. who have decided that the resourcing of the incident response team will be the responsibility of the IT department, while the manager in overall charge of incident response will be the IS manager, who will report through to the operations director. The essential reasoning behind this reporting line is that they already have responsibility for the various quality management systems, so should also be the director responsible for the Information Security Management System. However, legal and regulatory compliance and most aspects of corporate risk management are the responsibility of the Corporate Services department, headed by the legal director.

The IS manager is ISO27001 Auditor and Implementer trained but has been specifically recruited for his experience of running an incident response team. Although he has managed a team for several years, he has not set up a team from scratch. None of the rest of the IT or senior management have any IR experience. It is probably true to say that there will be some resistance to the introduction of this team. There are two key friction points:

- *Secondment of staff*: Even in a large organization it is most likely that some elements of the incident management group will be "associate" members in that they operate in a different area, but their specialist knowledge is called upon when required. This sort of relationship is not unusual with larger organizations for a range of reasons, but with incident management it may be that the associate may be required to focus on incident work, rather than their regular responsibilities, for some time. This can cause problems both with the associate, who is aware of a backlog of work building, and between managers as one is deprived of a member of staff.
- *Authority*: In larger organizations, it is common to find departments cherishing authority and being very unwilling to delegate that away even during an incident. There may be good reasons for that, as responsibility would stay with the "owner," but it can make it difficult to get action when the authority owner does not have a full understanding or appreciation of incident handling. This can slow down or, in worst-case situations, reduce the options for action.

Jade Ltd.

Jade Ltd. is a medium-sized data analytics organization. Their main property is situated in a major city with a second office focused on development work, sited on an out of town industrial estate. They also have a sales office in a serviced building in the regional capital.

Most of the data is extremely sensitive, as it comes from the financial, healthcare and government sectors. For this reason, they have a strong regulatory focus. Their customers are regulated by relevant bodies, so although there is no requirement for they themselves to so be, their customers are clear in their requirements that appropriate security policy and practices can be demonstrated.

Most of the IT is hosted at a data centre, but they have an internal IT manager with a staff of four to deal with local issues. Nobody in this team has any specific security expertise, so an experienced incident manager could be recruited.

Jade Ltd. decided to develop incident response capability after a close competitor was severely compromised, and has been critically damaged, by a fraudster who stole, and after an unsuccessful attempt at blackmail, then published a customer database.

A key challenge for Jade Ltd. is going to be the design of the incident response process and then linking that to education of the workforce. The event that was the trigger to this investment can only be handled effectively if staff can identify potential issues and know what the reporting procedures are. With incidents that manifest in technical symptoms, the route to the IT helpdesk is well trodden for most staff; they know who to call and the sort of help they can expect. However, the attack on the rival contained a significant social engineering element and this can be harder for staff to recognise and then further stretched to know the trigger point for reporting.

Because of the sensitive nature of the data they are handling, and the likely risk tolerance of the customer, Jade Ltd. are going to need to not only make staff aware of the system for handling incidents, but be able to demonstrate that the awareness training and communication is effective. The increasing sophisticated nature of attacks on this sort of data means that resistance to threat needs to be part of the operational culture within Jade Ltd. This can be challenging for any organization, as it requires both awareness education and re-enforcement amongst all staff, up to and including senior staff. As Jade Ltd. is quite small, stories of senior staff working around security guidelines will spread fast and undermine the general attitude of secure working that they need to adopt.

Because of the size of this organization, the IT manager initially responsible for the incident response actually has an advantage over their counterpart in Amber Inc. because they report directly to the board rather than through a reporting chain.

5
AND WHAT IS A SECURITY INCIDENT?

Houston, we have a problem.

Delivered by Tom Hanks as Jim Lovell in Apollo 13
1989

Information in this chapter:

- Recognising an event or incident
- Grading incidents
- Defining an incident
- Legal and regulatory meanings of "incident"
- Business continuity

Introduction

In films and television, we know when an incident is approaching. Lights flash, alarms sound, the accompanying musical score builds tension and people shout at each other or into phones. In the real world, as in the actual event of the explosion on Apollo 13, the awareness comes somewhat after the actual incident, so the actual quote was "Houston, we've had a problem."

The conclusion of many enquiries into incidents, such as the Hillsborough Stadium disaster of 1989, often include statements along the lines of the incident should have been anticipated given events leading up to it or that the early reaction to the incident was slow or inadequate. The question of defining when an action or concern becomes an "incident" requiring special action, can be hard to call.

If we take the example of the loss of a credit card, there can be a significant gap between some awareness of potential loss and the

25

formal reporting of the loss to the card provider. If the card alone is missing and not the wallet (which might indicate theft), how long should the user search before contacting the issuing authority to cancel the card? Even though new cards are generally issued within a working week, its absence for even a few days can be very inconvenient, so we often delay declaring as an incident the loss of a card.

Recognising an Event or Incident

So, one of the hardest things in incident management is actually recognizing when an incident has occurred. Many security incidents do not have even potentially noticeable impacts until long after the initial incident has occurred. For example, the loss of a USB key containing sensitive data might only be noticed when it is reported in the press. Hacker attacks might only be noticed when they access a particularly sensitive device or when an operating system update closes the vulnerability they are using. Even malware infections are not always obvious. As well as often not being easily detected until release of the relevant signature, many are now relatively subtle and difficult to detect by their behavior.

One of Matthew's most surreal incidents was initiated by a request for the admin password for a security-marked bank computer that had been bought on eBay. The purchaser of the stolen machine was a police officer (not one from a High-Tech Crime Unit).

Defining an Incident

There are a number of different ways of defining incidents. ISO27001 has:

> a single or a series of unwanted or unexpected information security events that have a significant probability of compromising business operations and threatening information security

It also introduces the concept of "security events":

> identified occurrence of a system, service or network state indicating a possible breach of information security policy or failure of safeguards, or a previously unknown situation that may be security relevant

A reasonable way to think of security-relevant information is what reaction you would expect to have.

- *Event*: Something detected and (hopefully) recorded by a security enforcing function. This may be indicative of something going wrong or, more commonly, of something going right. A useful example is a user getting their authentication details wrong. Most often, this is just because of mistyping or a recent password change.
- *Issue*: Something that requires a trivial reaction. This may be automated or scripted, but is unlikely to require any significant decision making. If our user from the previous example continues to get their password wrong, they will usually quickly be locked out and then they will need to get their password reset.
- *Incident*: What this book is all about. A manager or team will need to take decisions on response reactions, often based on incomplete information. Where this separates from the previous level will very much depend on your organization and its experience. Extending the previous analog – you might want to treat a repeated authentication failure against a sensitive resource – the board shared files or HR departmental file server, as an incident, rather than waiting for inappropriate access to occur.
- *Crisis*: Different from an incident only in degree. Where the impact or potential impact of an incident is so severe that good corporate governance requires executive management to be involved in the decision making process.

Obviously, the size of your organization and the maturity of your incident response team will make a very significant difference to how you handle things, as will your industry sector. A rash of spam is unlikely to be a considered even as an issue for most businesses but could impact the customer experience for an ISP or where the customer-facing services share bandwidth with the mail-server.

Experience can quickly drive things from crisis down to incident and even then down to issue. Phishing attacks are a good example. In the first of these Matthew dealt with, the business were represented by a Board director. Difficult questions were considered about whether internet banking simply needed to be turned off.

Shortly thereafter, responsibility and a credible amount of authority were delegated to the duty incident manager and a representative from the internet banking team. After a couple of years, the majority of attacks were being dealt with by the duty incident technician, who only informed the duty manager once an attack had been dealt with or if it was different in some substantive manner.

Grading Incidents

The incident continuum does deal with incidents in very broad terms of their impact on the business, so the most important grading is in terms of incident priority.

A useful scale may be as follows:

1. *Record only*: Although it is clear that there has been a security incident, no action will be taken unless requested by the business.
2. *Low priority*: Incident will be progressed if team resources permit.
3. *Standard priority*: Incident will be investigated but may not be immediate priority.
4. *High priority*: Incident will be investigated and resources will be taken from other on-going incidents if necessary.

Few incidents will end up in the outer levels, certainly until you are more sure of yourself. Quite a lot of incidents that get assigned to level 1 will be minor malware infections (just a few devices, mostly handled by the workstation AV) or low level employee investigations.

A large number of managers are surprisingly prurient and you will get requests for investigations without significant indications of serious wrongdoing. There will indeed be occasions where you need to investigate employees, but you need to be careful that you have sufficient and documented justification for any activities. Within the territory of Council of Europe members, employee privacy at work is protected under Article 8 of the European Charter of Human Rights. Getting to know the investigations and disciplinary side of your HR team and their external legal advisors is a very good idea, particularly if your team will be working in or, worse, across multiple jurisdictions.

It is also worth considering, if you are in a large organization, having an "executive interest" flag just as a reminder. Low priority incidents should remain, officially, low priority,* but may require more attention or simply updating because somebody important is particularly (reasonably or otherwise) interested in them. Quite often, this is because external parties will report incidents to a publicly well-known member of the executive, rather than involving people close to them. Some of the more interesting† of Matthew's incidents came that way.

Legal and Regulatory Meanings of "Incident"

There are a number of jurisdictions, regulatory authorities or compliance frameworks that have their own definition of "security incident" that are not necessarily congruent with those your business would choose if it was free to do so.

Particularly in the cases of pornographic material and personal information losses or releases, many jurisdictions have quite specific laws or guidance on what constitutes an incident (or, sometimes, an offence) and what you must do about it. Although some security frameworks such as ISO27001 are not particularly prescriptive, others such as PCI-DSS are much more so. Additionally, contractual obligations and, increasingly, cyber-insurance requirements, may also constrain your freedom of activity.

This isn't an area where, without knowing your market sector, your customer base and the regions you operate in (and under which jurisdictions' laws your contracts are placed) much more advice can be offered than:

- Be careful.
- Make sure you are aware of new business opportunities before the contracts are signed.
- Know some friendly and competent lawyers.
- Keep up to date with all standards and sector regulations that apply to you.

---

* But note our earlier definition of Level 1 incidents. The executive is "the business."
† Often in the Chinese sense. The interminable Australian Nun (over three years) and the "This isn't a bank, it's a fish and chip shop" incidents spring to mind.

Business Continuity

Availability, as far as most security people are concerned, is an inherent part of the classical security triad. However, in many if not most organizations, availability problems are dealt with under the business continuity process, which usually belongs to operations or IT, rather than to security.

Security incident management needs to ensure, however, that they are fully involved in the business continuity (and its big brother, disaster recovery) process.

Case Studies

Amber Inc.

Amber Inc.'s issues largely derive from the fact their business spans multiple jurisdictions. It is also important for a multinational company such as Amber Inc. to ensure that they meet regulatory and contractual requirements which govern the differing regions in which they work with particular reference to any sensitive and regulated sectors that apply in the different regions.

The guidelines for defining incidents should be formally recorded and available to all relevant personnel. This should be a key document in any table-top exercises or workshop training, along with details of any relevant legal or regulatory requirements, ensuring any changes in these requirements are incorporated in timely fashion.

Jade Ltd.

Jade Ltd. is small enough that they are unlikely to need to develop a detailed formal taxonomy for incidents. It is very important that senior management and those who have operational responsibility for dealing with incidents have a united definition of an "incident" with particular reference to operational risks and requirements. Given the outsourcing of much of their internet-facing services, they will have to work closely with their bank, ISP and the data centre to ensure that both contractual provisions and practical arrangements meet their business mandatory requirements and are pragmatic given the limited staffing they will be able to offer the ISIRT. Their key concern is likely to be the protection of the sensitive information that they are handling. Their business continuity will focus on the integrity and availability of this information as core business requirements and tabletop exercises should help staff become familiar with the actions and recording of actions that are required by contract and regulation.

Further Reading

UK Information Commissioner's Guide, *Employment Practices Code* and the *Supplementary Guidance*, particularly Part 3, "Monitoring at Work."

6

THE INCIDENT TIMELINE

The Road goes ever on and on
Down from the door where it began.
Now far ahead the Road has gone,
And I must follow, if I can,
Pursuing it with eager feet,
Until it joins some larger way
Where many paths and errands meet.
And whither then? I cannot say.

J. R. R. Tolkien
Fellowship of the Ring, Chapter 1

Information in this chapter:

- The eye of the storm – surviving in the centre of an incident
- Stages of an incident – gaining control through insight
  - Notification
  - Assessment
  - Investigation
  - Recovery
  - Closure
- Post-incident review

Introduction

As with many other things in life, incidents tend to follow a reasonably predictable pattern. You will, of course, have noticed the hedging in that sentence – some incidents will race through fast enough that you are barely sure they have hit all the steps. Others will plod through sufficiently slowly that, as they move to the next phase, you've almost forgotten about them. Particularly annoying ones will dance around the pattern, leaping backwards and forwards like an Irish dancer.

However, if you keep (or at least try) a track of where each incident is in its own pattern, it will help you to understand the possible next developments in the incident and to prioritise resource allocation between incidents.

Although a more formal model will be developed later in the chapter, in plain English, you will see that the pattern is fairly logical:

- Something happens (or is alleged to have happened).
- Your organization finds out about it.
- It is reported through to the incident management department (or another area of the business that can begin to do something with the information).
- You verify whether it is something you can or should be doing something about.
- You establish the business's priorities in dealing with the incident (although noting that these may take some time to be established).
- You attempt to investigate, fix or otherwise deal with the issue.
- New information, additional resources, business priorities and a host of other variables mean that you vary your activities in response.
- Eventually, whether because the incident is resolved to your satisfaction or, often, because additional activities are unlikely to improve matters to any significant extent.
- Ideally, you review the progress of events to see if there were any aspects of the way things were handled to see if there are suggestions to do things more effectively in future cases.

The Basics

So, taking those steps and combining some and splitting out investigations and recovery, as they are often the responsibility of different technical teams, you can re-work that pattern in to the stages of a simple but formal system:

- Notification
- Assessment

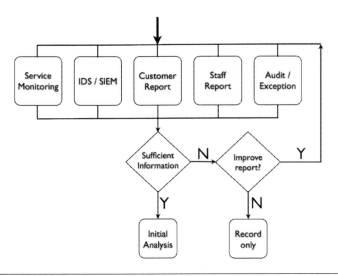

Figure 6.1 Example notification process.

- Investigation
- Recovery
- Closure
- Post-incident review

Notification

There are many ways of being notified of an incident. Some of them are indicated within the flowchart, but there will undoubtedly be others (Figure 6.1).

In many cases, the incident event will be immediately obvious as soon as it commences – a communications outage (e.g. an equipment failure or a line cut) or a phishing attack. In some cases, you might have signature or other controls that detect the attack, but possibly only after the initial attack, when there is a relevant signature update. In other cases, you may need to wait until there is an overt impact from the incident, such as logic bombs. In other cases, as with most financial frauds, an attack will only be detected if sufficient attention is paid to post-event or exception auditing.*

---

* In the days before online viewing of credit card accounts, your first report of a potential fraud, unless the account went over-limit, may have not been until the account holder got around to checking their monthly statement. Even an extremely conscientious card user who checked their statement the moment they received it may have been suffering from fraud for over a month.

Notifications can come by telephone, email, through your customer-facing call centres, from your ISP, from specialist security systems such as SIEM (Security Incident and Event Monitoring) applications or simple monitoring of boundary (internal or external) security devices.*

Traditional hacking, as an example, can fall in to any of the notification categories. Some hackers, particularly those with an activist motive, want you to know that you are being attacked. It is part of their attempt to persuade you to cease whatever it is they are objecting to. Many hacking attacks will upload tools for privilege escalation or further reconnaissance once they have their initial toehold in your network. In other cases, they may wish to conduct, for example, a website defacement on a notable date, which is common in politically motivated attacks. This doesn't mean that they attack on that date. They may well prepare a number of sites days or weeks in advance, gaining the necessary control, and only instantiate the defacement at their chosen significant moment. On the other hand, many financially motivated hackers will look to maintain surreptitious control for as long as they are benefiting from their crimes. Both technical and financial audits, combined, may be necessary to catch a crook who has managed to gain privileges to your online payments processing engine.

When Mastercard Secure and Verified By Visa were introduced, Matthew's team started to receive numerous reports from concerned customers, suspicious of the emails they were receiving from the external company that were providing these services for his employer. If you compared the emails to the generation of phishing attack emails that were prevalent at the time, they were very similar and broke many of the guidelines that had been agreed between the security, marketing and retail areas of the bank. It is essential to ensure that any of your suppliers who may have direct contact with your customers – as examples, independent quality assurance surveys or marketing agencies – are contracted to and monitored that they obey the same, or very similar, rules for email construction that you have established for your brands. Customer facing communication must be clear and obey basic security rules so as not to reduce the likelihood that customers will be alerted to a fraudulent communication and thereby notify the organisation.

---

* This one is rarely conclusive, hence why SIEM tools, with their more comprehensive feeds from server and other logs and correlation engines, are now increasingly prevalent in larger organizations.

The most important lesson is to make it easy for people to notify suspicious events. The default reaction should be to notify and nobody should be discouraged from or penalised for notifying something that bothers them. Reporting methods and any instructions you wish to put in place on what must, what should, and what should not (unless there are suspicious circumstances) be notified needs to form part of your employee education. Those employees with direct customer contact, such as helpdesks, telesales, account managers and similar, should receive further training to ensure that they are able to get sufficient information from a concerned customer to make a comprehensive report to your incident management team.

If the circumstances of your business and the frequency of attacks, particularly those directed at subverting your customers, warrants it, you may wish to establish reporting channels for your customers to directly report incidents. Most banks, as an example, now have an email address for customers to report phishing emails. Amongst other reasons, these emails are generally targeted (if they are targeted at all) at your customers, rather than your staff, so this is a good way to get the earliest practical warning at very little cost.*

Assessment

There is a sequence of simple questions that need to be considered in the initial assessment of any report of a potential incident (Figure 6.2):

1. Is this an information security relevant issue or is there a different team that are more capable of dealing with the issue?
   a. You are likely to have specialist teams for dealing with Data Subject Access Requests (for EEA companies or those in ones with similar data protection legislation), media inquiries and customer complaints.
   b. Equally physical security incidents (lost and found items, petty vandalism, burglary) may have a different reporting

---

* It is also worth establishing an auto-responder thanking the customer for the email and noting that they may be contacted by the Incident Management Team if there are special circumstances relevant to the email. You may also want to put the contact details for the Online Fraud team in to that email, in case the customer has actually suffered from a fraud.

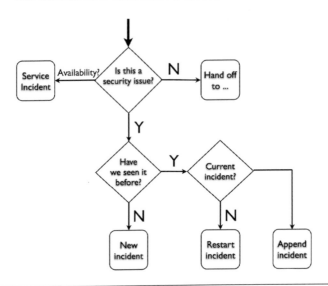

Figure 6.2   Initial assessment.

line, as also may fraud reports, despite both potentially
having information security components.*

2. Even if it is an information security issue, particularly where
the main impact is on the availability of one or more services,
should this be dealt with by the Service Incident (ITIL,
ISO20000) management process with security advice, rather
than by the security incident team?

3. If it is an information security event, does it meet your
corporate policy for being considered as an incident? Of
course, you may not have sufficient information to make that

---

* The most "ah, not us, really" report Matthew's team ever received was from an elderly
lady whose husband, a retired employee of the bank, had just died. His will and other
critical documents had been stored in a safety deposit box at the branch he used to
manage but all the telephone numbers had been rationalized to centralized call-
centres, where there wasn't an appropriate script to deal with this sort of problem. So,
somehow, the lady (in, by this time, a state of understandable and obvious distress)
ended up speaking to one of Matthew's deputies on the security incident hotline.
Needless to say, the right thing to do in that situation, whilst not recording it as a
security incident, was to take charge of the situation, find the appropriate responsible
manager and make sure they called the lady with whatever information would be
necessary to sort her situation out. And you should ensure that there is a check a day
or so later that things were as okay as they could be in this sad situation, which is
what happened.

judgement at this stage, in which case it should be recorded as a potential incident and more information may come to light later which would allow you to close the incident or to flag it up for further investigation.*

4. If you decide it is an incident, you should then decide whether this notification is of a new incident. A notification could be:
   a. More information relevant to a current, on-going incident.
   b. Stale information relevant to a closed incident.
   c. New information showing that a closed incident should be reopened.
   d. Or, indeed, a report of a separate, new incident that should therefore be opened?

In any case, the presumption should be to treat a report as a new incident, unless it is clear that any of the earlier conditions apply. If it later turns out to be one of the others, your recording system should be capable of allowing you to merge the two incidents.

In far too many cases, investigation of one incident throws up evidence of other incidents. Particularly, in Matthew's unfortunate experience, when you start looking at staff email. It was a rare case where you didn't find, somewhere in any email investigation, pornography or other Acceptable Use Policy violations. The circumstances of the particular cases will determine whether the new tangential information should be treated as part of the same investigation or spun off in to a new case. Your particular prioritisation process should help to make this clear, as would the degree to which the cases or the people involved differ. One particularly complex investigation in to inappropriate release of market-sensitive company data spun off several porn investigations, an investigation in to possibly criminal abuse of privileged network accounts, and police-led investigations in to computer misuse (i.e. hacking) and even an attempted murder.

If you have decided that you do indeed have an incident to deal with, you then need to apply your prioritisation scheme, which should then drive the next stage of the activities.

---

* Doing this allows you to monitor whether your reporting mechanisms are asking sufficient or the correct questions to make an accurate and rapid determination for the majority of reports.

Also, here, you may separate your incidents in to any different categories you may have, such as service incidents (often to do with availability), business continuity incidents, and standard and "special handling" information security incidents.

These latter two stages will be addressed in more detail in the next chapter.

Investigation

This is, understandably, often the most complex part of the incident management process, especially as it involves considerations of your legal rights, and those of the people you are investigating; fine grained judgements on technical issues, often based on partial and inadequate information; and, usually, considerable pressure from the business to resolve the issue so that they can get back to normal operating and, in many cases, making money.

As noted earlier, it will often happen in parallel with the recovery stage (unless you are in a situation where you are required or have decided to conduct a digital forensic investigation and, sometimes, even then.) The different priority for resource between investigation and recovery is one of the most difficult judgements that need to be made. However, unless there is a legal or contractual obligation to conduct a detailed investigation, this is a decision that the incident manager should not just leave up to the business but should insist that the business take and formally document that they have done so.

In some cases, you will have sufficient resources or the appropriate tools and data* to conduct both streams separately without having to prioritise one or the other. Normally, however, there will be a conflict. And, normally, the business will insist on recovery taking priority as soon as possible, so you need to ensure that as much data is collected for subsequent analysis, before it is over-written by the recovery activities.

The cyclic nature of the investigations process will be covered in Chapter 8.

---

* Email investigations can often be conducted on a restore to an investigations server of the latest backups for the relevant email servers, rather than interfering with the live email servers, most of whose users are unlikely to be connected to your incident. Please note, however, that, especially if there is suspicion that a criminal offence may have been committed, that you are fully aware of the rules of evidence in the relevant jurisdiction(s).

Recovery

If you are in a pure information security role, recovery is unlikely to be a core activity for your team. However, it will draw away any additional IT and some external resources that would have otherwise been available for your investigations work.

If, of course, you are part of the IT department, then this is a, if not the, key part of your role.

The business is likely to want service restored as closely as possible to the condition they were in immediately before the incident impact was noticed. However, it is important that sufficient investigation is conducted to determine when the initial incident occurred, as there may have been a progressive deterioration in capability or damage to resources, that was only apparent once it reached a critical threshold or an infrequent business process was invoked.

In serious cases, recovery will be dependent on the availability of reliable, comprehensive and recent data back-up. This means that not only is it essential that backups are taken regularly and correctly, but also that they are regularly tested to ensure that they are effective and cover the range of systems and data that you expect. This will involve actually conducting restores as part of the test, ideally on to non-live systems in case there is an issue. Where appropriate, full environment restores can be tested in a controlled environment as part of business continuity or disaster recovery exercises.

Your business processes, technology and the precise impact(s) of the incident will drive the nature and specifics of recovery actions. Unfortunately, these will therefore be sufficiently varied that it is difficult to give anything other than the most general advice.

Pre-Recovery Checks

Before undertaking recovery, it is essential that the following are established:

- That there is no legal or contractual bar to you potentially destroying evidence relating to the incident.
- That investigations actions have either been stopped or will not be affected.

- When you will be recovering the systems or data too, and what business significant or critical information will have changed between that time and the time of the incident, and at least beginning to plan how this delta will be recovered.
- That if the recovery will cause a temporary outage, this has been agreed with the business units affected.
- That all necessary backup tapes or other media are available.
- If the recovery fails, that there is a roll-back or other fall-back process.

If some of these aspects cannot be achieved, it may be possible to recover on to a cold-standby BCP platform or a system re-purposed from a development or test role.

Closure

As will be discussed in more detail later, eventually the investigation will eventually stop generating new information or, for continuous or repeated attacks, the attack will cease. This means that recovery actions will be complete or, at very least, significantly underway. However, there are no further actions for or requirements from the IR staff.

Of course, where additional investigations have spun off an initial incident report and the subsequent investigations work, these should be treated as separate incidents if possible, thereby allowing them to be closed independently of the main incident and vice versa.

Once it becomes apparent that an incident has reached a natural conclusion, unless the incident is minor or has been very brief, it is worth considering taking an explicit pause to catch breath, have some food, or even a night's sleep. After that, if things still look okay, the incident may, if there has been no recurrence or additional consequent (*concomitant?*) impact, be formally closed. Declaring an incident closed should normally be the responsibility of the nominated (or on-shift) incident manager.

It should be noted that there may still be secondary activities on-going outside of the incident management team, such as disciplinary or legal processes or customer or regulatory communications. These may involve the team or specific members in presenting evidence but, important though these activities may be, they rarely have the urgency explicit in the initial incident response.

Post-Incident Review

Unless you are repeatedly subject to very similar incidents, in which case they will tend to become more and more like "issues" as you develop a methodology for dealing with them, it is appropriate, even necessary, to conduct a formal post-incident review (Figure 6.3).

In these cases, it is essential that there is a dispassionate review of the conduct of the incident, after the fire is well and truly out, the smoke damage has been cleaned and repaired and, to stretch the analogy somewhat, the insurance cheque has cleared. In other words, at a sufficient remove from the incident itself that everybody is rested, the day-job work queue is no longer backed up, and people can be wholly rational about what happened.

We refuse to apologise for repeating throughout this book that these reviews will not be effective if the organization does, or is believed to, treat them as witch-hunts. There may indeed be somebody who legitimately deserves the blame for the incident and its various impacts (and this may even be clear from the prior investigations work). However, there are other ways of dealing with such situations – through the organisation's disciplinary process or the civil or criminal law, if necessary.

The purpose of the post-incident review is to see if there are any lessons to be learned by the incident management team. Learning points can encompass many aspects including:

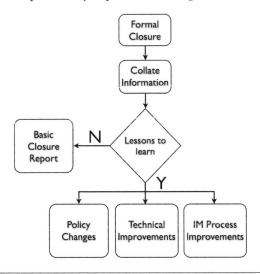

Figure 6.3 Basic post-incident review.

- Excessive delays in initial notification of the incident.
- Insufficient information gathered to make the proper triage decisions at the assessment point.
- Inexperience or training gaps amongst the incident response team – for example, no forensics technician available when one was required.
- Information sources that were overlooked, late in presenting, or did not provide the information that they were expected to, or on the positive side, unexpected information sources that provided material information.
- Communications problems – whether within the team, with partner organisations, or between the team and senior management or specialist advisors.
- Equipment faults or shortages.
- A new equipment one of the partner organisations brought that would improve future incident handling.*
- Gaps in the documented processes – possibly an incident involving a different legal jurisdiction for which you didn't have an available advisor.
- Decisions made that, with 20/20 hindsight, were probably not the best; remembering that prevarication in an incident scenario is almost always as bad as a wrong decision.

This vital aspect of incident response – your continuous improvement process – is dealt with in more detail in Chapter 20.

Revealing the Case Studies

Amber Inc.

Because of the multinational nature of Amber Inc., there may be a range of different incident types and also methods of notification, while the interpretation of the notification and the transference into action is more likely to be taken centrally, especially if the incident is serious.

One of the most important notification routes is the call centre, which includes phone and email and also chat. Again, if these are

---

* Or, in other words, a shiny new toy that you must, must have. (Gollum!)

run centrally in one country, it will be important for communication staff to have some training in identifying incident notifications in their contact with people from other countries than their own. Also, the "script" that communications staff have in helping with problems will need to highlight the sort of information that may indicate the problem might be sufficiently serious to be pushed up to a supervisor for further review.

Jade Ltd.

Jade Ltd. does not have to have the same customer contact that Amber Inc. does, so their challenge, while including the need for good communication, is in relation to outside services that support their system. Crucially, IT is provided and managed externally, so it is important that these providers both understand weak points where there is the potential for a security incident, and what actions are required of them. This is particularly true as most of the most serious security threats to Jade Ltd. are likely to relate to their IT system. Whether that is a breach of security, a loss of access or a corruption of data there is a strong possibility that the problem will first be identified by the external IT team. How the incident is dealt with in the first instance, as well as when and what sort of contact with Jade Ltd. is required has to be mutually understood and agreed. As threats change, the success of that early stage handling and contact will need to change, with indication of the need to do that most likely being identified in the post-incident review.

7
TYPES AND PRIORITIES

Organizing is what you do before you do something, so that when you do it, it is not all mixed up.

A. A. Milne

Information in this chapter:

- Prioritisation of incidents
- Categorisation of incidents
- Identifying the likely cause and impact of the incident
- The importance of clear communication

Introduction

There are many different types of incidents with an information security context or impact and depending on the nature and culture of your business and the degree to which an incident has affected it, there will be a number of categories and priorities that you will wish to assign. Any schema should be easy to understand but tailored to meet the overall structure of your business, particularly regarding lines of authority, as well as encompassing any metrics which you are required to collect.

You will also need to accommodate any core organizational requirements or peculiarities. It is helpful to be able to identify incidents which are linked to legal or disciplinary cases, those of regulatory significance, or are of interest to one or more of the corporate executives for other reasons.

It is also useful to split off investigations where there are allegations or suspicion of staff or customer malfeasance, as this type of incident, especially if the suspicions turn out to be incorrect, needs to be handled in a much more circumspect manner.

This is very much "different strokes for different folks," so there is definitely no correct or even advisable way to arrange things. Apart from the splits between security and service incidents – primarily handled by different teams although with appropriate representation on the incident management groups where there were wider concerns – and between standard and the "special handling" security incidents, Matthew had the following flags available on the incident management system:

- Executive interest
- Communications
- Regulatory concern

The latter two were to ensure that the appropriate media relations* or risk departments were kept informed of any significant changes to the investigation and, obviously, the final results, if any.

Cases where law enforcement were actively involved were sufficiently rare that these were handled individually, under the wider "special handling" process.

Flowchart

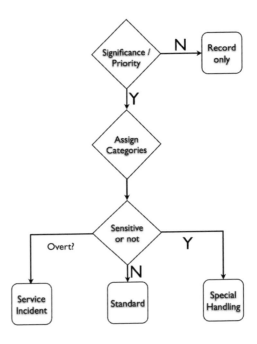

---

* The top level media relations team were called "group communications," hence the slight ibowdlerization.

Prioritisation

Simple Schema

How much of a prioritisation scheme you wish to put in place is very much going to depend on the number of incidents you have (the more, the more nuanced a scheme will be required) and any statutory or contractual requirements.

Any scheme will need to distinguish between those incidents that it is necessary to record, but for which no substantive action is intended, and the various priorities of incident that must, will, or may be investigated.

The following is merely an example of a relevant taxonomy which combines both types of grading:

- Priority 1 incidents must be investigated, and resource will be re-assigned from lower priority investigations.
- Priority 2 incidents will be investigated.
- Priority 3 incidents may be investigated where resource permits.
- Priority 4 incidents will not be investigated unless deemed essential by the affected business area management or the group head of security.
- Priority 5 incidents are recorded for statistical purposes and will not be investigated.

In this scheme, where there is, as yet, insufficient information to properly assess an incident, it was rated at priority 2 until enough information is available. If no further information is forthcoming, after a set period (48 hours may be a reasonable timescale) the incident could then be downgraded to priority 4 or 5.

Also, remember that incident priority is not fixed once it has been set. An incident where somebody alleges that two people are emailing pornography to each other, where the complainant is acting on hearsay rather than actually having caught them at it, might rate assignment as priority 3.* However, if the initial investigation discovered hardcore pornography would rate raising the priority to at least a priority 2.

---

* This, clearly, very much depends on the culture of the organization. If this is an inappropriate example, you might construct one around chain letters or other breaches of the organization's acceptable use policy, with actual fraud or threats of violence as the indicator that the priority must be raised.

Discovery of illegal pornography – child pornography or, in some jurisdictions, "extreme pornography" (however that is defined) – would rate raising it immediately to priority 1.

Equally, an incident may be downgraded. Suspected pornography, to continue the example, may be discovered to be "inappropriate for the workplace" imagery – possibly the lesser offence of misuse, rather than abuse, of systems.

Privacy and Investigations

It is also worth noting the complex relationship between security incident investigation and Human Resources and disciplinary practice. Depending on the privacy and employment law in the jurisdiction you are investigating,* you will probably need to have suspicion of a certain level of misconduct before invasive techniques can be justified. With legal advice, set an appropriate threshold or set of thresholds and ensure that your team stick to them or, where there is pressure to act outside them, specific legal advice is taken.†

If your remit spans multiple jurisdictions, make sure that any differences (including those mandated by the law) are fully justified in the team instructions.

It is important that line managers continue to manage in accordance with organizational policy. They may very well demand security investigations, even digital forensics, be used to uncover evidence of time-wasting or similar low impact breaches of organizational codes of conduct or other policies, but this is rarely an efficient use of resources. Where there is a requirement for security involvement – for example, where a low-level disciplinary has now reached the stage where dismissal is a reasonable sanction if proven, and there is a requirement for robust evidence (i.e. for potential presentation at a subsequent Employment Tribunal or civil court case challenging the result of the disciplinary), then the level of information released to the line management or the deciding panel needs to be carefully managed

---

* This may very well differ from the one you are conducting the investigation in and the jurisdiction the evidence is resident in may be different again.

† Acting more leniently or more stringently in any one case may damage the legal acceptability of the actions, findings and punishments in other cases.

to ensure the minimum breach of privacy of the accused and to avoid breaching the privacy of any third parties.

The extent of managerial prurience was one of the more unpleasant surprises for Matthew, moving back from a small consultancy into the large organization culture. Numerous times, merely because somebody was beneath them in the hierarchy, managers requested access to the personal emails* of their staff. Even if there is a suspicion of significant wrong-doing, this is rarely the correct course of action. If an investigation is warranted, then the incident response team should conduct the investigation and only emails relevant to the allegations, redacted where necessary and, ideally, merely statistics and other metadata should be released to line management or departmental HR staff.[†]

Additional Concerns

Although you might consider an incident to have a specific priority, there may be other bits of the business that either view it as significantly more serious or regardless of severity, need to be informed.

Many large organizations have a team of people who respond to public complaints sent to the chairman, CEO or other senior executives. Regardless of how trivial the complaint is, these will almost always need a formal response back to the complaints team so that they, in turn, can respond to the complainant. Equally, many organizations operate in industries where there is a regulatory or statutory complaints system. Again, these will usually require a formal response, often within prescribed time limits, regardless of whether the complaint is trivial or not.

If an incident is obvious to or affects customers or the wider public, you will need to involve your customer and media relations teams (who may be the same people). If the incident is of regulatory significance, you

---

* Low level (i.e. non-disruptive to work or systems) personal use of email, web and corporate telephony was generally permitted by the AUP in force at the time. In fact, one of Matthew's staff once had to use their work mobile for an extensive international call and tried to repay the cost. After much deliberation, it was decided that it would be more expensive to process the charge-back than would be recouped.

† This was within the UK. As noted earlier, jurisdictions do vary enormously in their employment rights laws and in the expectation of privacy when using work systems for personal purposes.

may need to inform the team that manages the regulatory relationship. If the incident involves a crime, you may be required to or management may decide to, involve law enforcement. There should be a facility to note these and any similar factors within the incident recording system.

The first Distributed Denial of Service incident Matthew investigated did have a significant customer impact (i.e. a total outage of part of the customer-facing proposition). One of the largest customers of that particular area was one of the UK's most popular (and vicious) online business technology websites, "The Register," more commonly known, after both its logo and the attitude of some of its reportage as "Vulture Central." Watching the careful crafting of the customer relations messages (and then correcting them to remove any technical inaccuracies that had crept in) was both entertaining and educational.

If you have a digital forensics capability and if you sometimes use external consultants to assist in your investigations, you may also want to be able to flag if these have been required. One of the key uses of incident metrics is to justify to budget holders the requirement for maintaining or even increasing expenditure in forthcoming years. Knowing what the requirement has been for resources, particularly the expensive ones, is vital in being able to structure a rational budget submission.

One of the surprises for Matthew when he was working for the bank was the enthusiasm for growing the computer forensics capability despite a general attitude of budget restraint. Perhaps key to this, as well as the functionality it brought particularly to complex fraud investigations, was the rather "impressive" bill for the first forensic investigation conducted before his teams' equipment had arrived by an external consultancy. This was especially offensive to his boss at the time because the kit did arrive towards the end of the investigation and much of the difficult analysis work (rather than the time-consuming but not exactly taxing imaging work) was actually done by him and one of his deputies.

Incident Categories

As with priorities, categorisation is very much a matter for the requirements of the business. Your culture, regulatory environment, number of incidents and experience will all feed in to the number and variety of categories you wish to adopt.

Generally, broad categories are usually best with (if your incident recording system permits it) sub-categories underneath it. However, the important things are clarity and consistency. It must be reasonably obvious, if with a little training, what category or categories to assign to an incident, once you have enough information to make an informed decision. It is also extremely time-consuming to go back through your database to re-categorise incidents if you change the taxonomy or the way it is applied, as well as embarrassing to have to re-issue your historic weekly or monthly reports.

For example, both "external* attack" and "fraud" are very broad categories. Distributed denial of service attacks, classic hacking and advanced persistent threat are all external attacks, although very different in methodology, immediate impact and potential for brand or business damage in the longer term. Equally, fraud may be committed internally; by suppliers, partners or customers; or by known or unknown third parties. And the targets of the fraud you are seeing transiting your systems may be your own business, your business partners or even your customers.[†]

You may, of course, wish to allow incidents to be in multiple categories – both phishing attacks and spoof websites are both "external" and "fraud."

However, treating incidents in this way is likely to cause problems with all but the most comprehensive metrics reporting system. A phishing attack, as above, is clearly just one incident, but is it 50% fraud and 50% external attack, 99% one or the other and 1%, or anywhere in between. If multiple categories are required, a preferable option is to have a primary category and then additional categories which can then be allocated.

Cause and Impact

Matthew's preferred taxonomy style is based on a combination of the source and the potential impact(s) of the incident.

---

* "External" here referring to "outside the trusted network" rather than making any premature judgment about who is behind the attack.

[†] Not withstanding the interesting speculation, clearer in some jurisdictions than others, about who finally, legally bears the actual risk of the incidence of a successful fraud.

In this, "special handling" would be seen as a meta-category, whose purpose is mostly to restrict access to details of the incident to the minimum necessary personnel. If your system has sufficiently granular control of privileges, you may be able to allow management, audit and risk personnel to view metadata regarding the incident. For example, the incident reference number, date commenced, status, responsible incident manager and business unit(s) affected, but without allowing them to view the nature of the names of suspects or victims.

Incident Cause

Causes can be obvious or can be allocated as the investigation progresses. A sample taxonomy may consist of:

- Not yet assessed (obviously, the default choice)
- Unknown*
- External attack
- Compromise of partner/supplier
- Insider Attack
- Malware (possibly split in to "targeted" and "un-targeted")
- Acceptable use violation
- Equipment malfunction
- Process failure

Impacts

Equally, impacts can be unknown, obvious and, in many cases, multiple. Some examples are:

- Not yet assessed (again, the default)
- Nil†
- Financial loss. This can usefully be split in to:
  - Fraud
  - Significant recovery costs

---

* If an attack remains "cause unknown" on completion of the investigation, you might expect this to be explicitly commented upon in the post-incident review. Also note this is materially different from "other."

† This is a positive statement that there was no impact. Obviously, there would be some resource expended by the incident response team, but you can usefully consider this a sunk cost.

- Compensation/contractual or Service Level Agreement refunds
- Loss of income
- Customer/partner losses
- Fine (legal or regulatory)
- Loss of service*
- Formal complaint
    - Staff
    - Customer†
    - Partner
    - Third-party
- Confidential data release
    - Personal (customer or potential customer {e.g. marketing database})
    - Personal (staff)
    - Corporate
    - Other
- Deletion of or damage to significant data
- Regulatory censure (potential or actual)
- Court or tribunal sanction
- And, the ever popular "other"

KISS

At its full extent, the implementing the above recommendations would lead to quite a complicated taxonomy. If you are dealing with a small number of incidents per month or per year, you are unlikely to need to go anywhere near this far. In those cases, simply describing the incident in a brief, searchable text field may be sufficient. Also, if your initial incident response is through a general helpdesk before it gets to people with more specific training, you may wish to simplify or otherwise limit the options they are presented. "Unknown" or "not yet assessed" is more helpful than an incorrect categorisation.

If you are specifying an incident management system and you do not think you need a detailed taxonomy, remember to ensure that it

---

* As opposed to "Denial of Service," which is a cause!

† Again, any significant loss of customers would be expected to be highlighted in the PIR.

has sufficient flexibility to extend your environment if you require it in the future.

In fact, that is a good general rule for the selection of any incident recording or management technology – ensure it has more flexibility built in than you currently think you will ever need. More about this in Chapter 12.

Revealing the Case Studies

Amber Inc.

Amber Inc. has a number of reasons to be concerned about identifying and reporting and prioritising incidents. A prime one is that they supply a range of goods across a number of countries. They need to have customer service processes that not only suit the legal requirements, but also cultural issues. In some countries, such as parts of the USA, customers are well practiced in the skill of complaint. They know how to complain and what they expect to be a reasonable outcome. In other places, such as some parts of the UK, customers will build up to complaining; they will put up with a fault, and think on it until they reach a point where they can't handle the complaint for another moment.

Where these are complaints regarding good for sale then it is unlikely that the IT or IR team need to become involved. However, if the issue is with regard to a failure of IT, or a deliberate take-down, or denial of service attack on their online shop, then, particularly at peak times, the loss of business is potentially serious.

Where there are differences between the urgency of dealing with a type of incident, whether that is consistent across the countries they generally sell most, or whether it is specific to a region, there needs to be work conducted to agree priorities for the different scenarios. There also needs to be an override, where an event that might not usually be considered important or urgent.* Also in the course of the post-incident reviews (which will be discussed in more detail in Chapter 19), where the handling of the incident is reviewed in order to recognise effective actions, identifying areas where there were

---

* There being a difference between those two words that is often not recognised.

difficulties in order to adjust handling to make a similar attack in the future be dealt with more effectively.

Because Amber's Inc. business depends on customer sales, it is vital that any incidents that impact that are properly identified and prioritised, and that priorities and the actions that they trigger are understood by all in both the customer service team and the IR team.

Jade Ltd.

Because of the nature of the data that Jade Ltd. are processing any incident that impacts that data is going to be serious. However, even at that single level it is going to be necessary to identify the type of incident that is in play, and priorities that will better enable the efficient handling of the event. Also, because most of the IT operations are outsourced it is going to be necessary to ensure that they are also aware of key priorities for incidents involving their data. This will include such points as when an IR or IT manager from Jade Ltd. be made aware of an ongoing situation.

Because of the responsibility that Jade Ltd. still has for safe processing, even when this is outsourced it is still their responsibility to be aware of relevant incidents, and the easiest way of being able to describe a situation, especially in the early stage when the full extent of issue or impact may not be clear, a priority template can be quicker to use and leave IR staff to gather further information.

8

THE INVESTIGATION CYCLE

The world is a circle without a beginning,
And nobody knows where it really ends.
Everything depends on where you
Are in the circle that never begins.
Nobody knows where the circle ends.

Burt Bacharach
The World Is A Circle

Information in this chapter:

- Conflicting demands
- The cyclical model
- Investigative activities
- Restorative activities
- Monitoring and review

Introduction

Cyclic models have been all the rage for a considerable period of time. Colonel Boyd's "OODA loop"* and the Demming Quality Assurance Cycle† found in many ISO standards serve to highlight the need to modify your behaviour as the circumstances you are responding to and your desired goals change over time. Incident management is no different, and working with a semi-formalised cyclical model is often useful, particularly as additional information regarding the incident will often result in radical alteration to your proposed courses of action.

---

* Observe, Orientate, Decide, Act.
† Plan, Do, Check, Act. Occasionally seen as "Adjust" for the final stage.

In fact, the actual business of the investigation is often the most exciting bit of incident response. It is certainly the bit that most enthuses technical staff; the solving of knotty problems with partial information. Something (but not much) like a cross between crosswords and Soduko, all done under pressure and "on the clock."

However, it is rarely a simple linear exercise. Initial investigation will give you a partial view of some aspects of the problem, which will then allow you to direct further investigations work. Quite often, while your team are working hard at your command, you will receive more details about the problem which make it obvious you have been diving down the rabbit hole for the past few hours and you need to re-direct the team.

The first DDoS Matthew and his team investigated, as already mentioned, was interesting. The red herring in this case was the lack of extortion emails. By that time, the criminals had a well tried and understood technique – DDoS a gambling site 24 hours before a major event and try to force them to pay the "consultancy fee" before betting on the event had to close. This was, however, the first attempt, to our knowledge, to take down a major payments service provider.

Except no extortion demands arrived – none sent to the CEO, nor to the marketing director, nor to any of the other publicly known senior manager email accounts – either in the business or in the wider group. This was, for a couple of days, an apparently motiveless attack coming from a broad spectrum of the internet. Although various recovery actions were successfully put in place, the investigation aspect was stalled.

The problem turned out to be that the extortionist was targeting a payments page hosted by the PSP, but apparently on one of the PSP's customer's sites. And the extortion demands were going to the customer who was ignoring them, as they (a very small online store) were not seeing any impact to their systems and did not cotton on to the loss of business until they got the briefing emails from the PSP customer relations team.

Once we had the information from them, there were then problems with "clever ideas" from certain executives who, because of the business impact, were attending some of the incident meetings. But that's a different, later, issue.

Once you have a real idea of what the problem is, you then have to try to work out the solution. Often, the investigation requires you to look deeper than the minimum necessary to simply restore things to pre-incident functionality. It may require you to search for the culprit (whether that is accident, negligence or malice.) It may require you to propose a solution which will mitigate against or even prevent future similar attacks.

All this will be taking place under a changing background of requirements, of different priorities and urgencies, from the business you are trying to support.

Therefore, the issue becomes an iterative one – hopefully slowly spiraling in towards your target, rather than outwards, out of control.

Conflicting Demands of Initial Review, Detailed Investigation and Restoration

You should arrive at this stage of the incident process with a reasonable assessment of the priority and the context, if not yet the categorisation of the incident. If, as an example, the security incident has become apparent from within the context of a service, you may well have large amounts of information which has been gathered from that investigation.* On the other hand, you may merely have a brief complaint, passed from one of your call centres, from a less than technical customer.

With the limited resources available, there are three main options:

- Further initial review work to establish current impacts, categorisation and more accurate priorities, as well as whether or not the incident falls in to special handling or any of the special notification issues.
- Recovery or restoration.
- Detailed investigations:
  - Into the precise causes and impacts (especially if certain impacts require notification to regulatory authorities).

---

* Although without, necessarily, the ingrained cynicism and peculiar "left of field" viewpoint that are so valuable to the security investigator.

- Attempting to identify the attacker (if there is one or more than one).
- Considering the collection of evidence for disciplinary or legal action.

As has been previously noted, the business should have charge of directing the main priority between recovery and detailed investigation action, however, it is essential that the incident is properly understood, not least so any legally or contractually mandatory actions are taken in a timely and effective manner. This will require careful management of the business if the impact of the incident is currently severe.

It is worth appreciating that many organizations are particularly weak conceptually or practically in IT risk evaluation and management. A small service interruption now in order to prevent or strongly mitigate a possible larger future issue, may be entirely rational to an experienced IT risk manager, but is often wholly unacceptable to an organization where short term goals are perceived as prime. It takes both strong character and effective top cover, ideally at the executive level, for junior incident staff to insist on initiating or continuing any level of service disruption. Affected business or sales managers are rarely experts in the organization's legal obligations, even where these form part of standard contractual offerings.

The bottom line is this: If you do not yet know what is actually happening (forgetting about even proximate causes at this point, never mind distal or fundamental cause), it is almost always safer to act steadily but cautiously, rather than to dither or act dramatically.

Decisiveness is often a good characteristic of an incident manager, but it must be coupled with sufficient humility to both recognise where mistakes have been made and to take corrective actions. And, where appropriate (and, as you are in charge, it almost always is), a full and sufficient share of the blame.*

---

* "Sufficient" is often "all of it" or "so much of it that the difference isn't worth arguing over."

The Cyclical Model

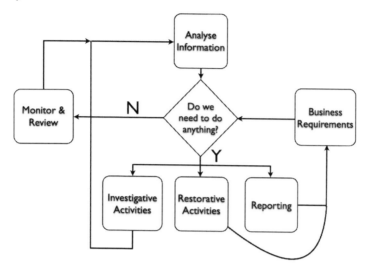

Generally, you will progress around this cycle in a series of phases, before exiting:

- *Discovery*: Where the focus is on understanding the impacts and implications of the incident.
- *Main effort*: Where the focus is discovering the mechanisms, details and causes of the incident.
- *Stabilisation*: Where the focus is on reverting to normal business and providing the necessary inputs to post-incident processes.

It should be noted, however, that this is not rigid, and the changes in the incident impacts, arrival of new or better information or analysis, and changes in business requirements or available resources can all move you rapidly back to earlier phases.

Often, in fact, movement between phases is only obvious in hindsight.

Analysis

The first step in the investigations process is to analyse all the information currently available. It is vital that you pause and work out, each and every time:

- What you know
  - What you actually know

- What you think you know
- What you are fairly sure you don't know but really ought to*
- What resources are available
- Whether or not there are any mandatory activities (legal regulatory or contractual)
- What constraints there are on your activities†
- What the ideal end points of the investigation will look like

Then you need to understand the level of pragmatism acceptable within the organization, taking in to account the current context. Depending on your local culture, an incident with a very significant impact may result in people being keen to try anything that might improve matters or people may retreat into established procedures.‡

Particularly with new types of incident, it is essential that participants in the response effort feel free to offer different interpretations of the information to hand and imaginative approaches to progressing the investigation or even solving the problem. In a strongly hierarchical organization or where there is considerable risk aversion, it is often difficult to persuade junior staff, who are often the most knowledgeable about the idiosyncrasies and foibles of particular technologies, to speak out. It is a critical part of the management of incident meetings to ensure that these people are given the time and the encouragement to voice their suggestions even if these are rejected after discussion.§

---

* We'll stop at this point just in case we start channeling Donald Rumsfeld. But, despite being mocked for it (About.com has it as one of their "25 Dumbest Quotes from the Bush Years"), his "known unknowns" versus "unknown unknowns" comment was actually not just sensible – if you take the time to listen to or read it carefully – but also, especially for a politician speaking about a complex subject, a remarkably clear explanation of the military intelligence problem. It is just as applicable to incident management.

† For example, these might include a change management process that requires permission for some restoration activities from a change board or emergency change controller.

‡ It is the former, of course, that is likely to have the most productive, technically, results. However, it may lead to all sorts of legal, regulatory and career troubles.

§ And especially when they are rejected, it is important after the event, to thank the people for coming up with their suggestions. Next time, they might provide the critical input to an incident but, if they are shouted down or otherwise discouraged, not only will they not try to speak up again, but the message will be passed on to their colleagues.

It is extremely galling to struggle to an acceptable solution for a particularly harsh incident, only for one of the junior people to pipe up and have a conversation with you something along the lines of:

> You shouldn't do that quite *that* way. If you change that and modify these settings here then it will work a lot faster.

> Oh, you've done this before have you?

> Well, yes, my MSc project was on this when it was still in beta and we used it a lot in my last job.

> Why didn't you say anything earlier?

> Well, you didn't ask *me!*

This is usually a failure of the incident management system and particularly the incident manager, not of the junior member of staff. You have to be especially particular when you are dealing with partner organizations that may have a different culture to yours. Remember that, as they see it, they may be dealing with a very important customer so be on their "best behavior," which may include not criticising or correcting you or members of your team.

The Business Requirement

It is essential to remember that incident response is not an aim in itself. Even if you are in a computing or software organization, you are there to support the delivery of the business. However, there are a very large range of desired business outcomes beyond the simplistic "just make it go away" and these will drive the whole thread of your progress.

Examples of typical business requirements, outside restoration, include:

- Providing sufficient evidence for law enforcement to be able to investigate and prosecute an attacker or fraudster.
- Collecting sufficient admissible evidence for your legal team to realistically expect to succeed in a civil case against an attacker.
- Gaining control of a domain that was used for a passing-off or "sucks" website.

- Collecting sufficient information to satisfy regulatory or contractual commitments – for example, for personal data breach cases, credit card information breaches for organizations subject to PCI-DSS or to satisfy the liability exclusion terms in service level agreements.
- Determining the proximate or underlying cause of an incident so that preventative or mitigating controls can be introduced or improved.

These should come where there is more than one and there almost always is with relative priorities – in both urgency and ultimate importance. These can be and ideally should be expressed in simple English.* Reasonable examples might include:

- We must have the fraud site shut down as soon as possible and we would like to gain control over the domain.†
- We have decided to report this extortion to the police, so you must keep detailed, admissible evidence; however, our urgent requirement is for some degree of service to be restored to customers.
- Our critical concern is discovering why this has happened; we are prepared to tolerate absolutely necessary disruption of service for up to 24 hours; if you believe more time will be required, we will need to move to off-line investigations.

It is also worth remembering that conforming to local norms, cultural or technical, is a perfectly valid business requirement. As would be any additional work necessary to keep the investigation within the bounds of political sensitivities. This is especially critical in larger organizations, particularly where reporting lines vary between the different teams involved or where external parties are conducting some of the work.

---

* Other languages are, of course, available.

† Criminals are very good at choosing domain registries and registrars with lax terms and conditions and worse enforcement of them. Regardless, if you complain to a registrar that a domain is being used fraudulently and by the time they get around to having a look there is nothing there (because you have efficiently had the hosting company delete the web pages or virtual server). They are unlikely to be keen to help you. Keep appropriate evidence.

"Monitoring the Incident" versus "Doing Something"

- Do you actually need to do anything?
- Or, if you clearly do, do you yet know enough to make a sensible stab at what it should be?

It is a common complaint of the media interaction with politics that 24-hour news with an hourly or half-hourly cycle often forces politicians to knee-jerk responses: doing something merely to be seen to be responding to the issue. Hastily thought out "somethings" are rarely "the right thing" and often not a "wise thing" or even a "helpful thing." High-profile incidents can generate similar pressures within organizations.*

Sometimes, you must have the courage to insist that you simply need more information or to continue with your existing activities. It is not essential to come out of every incident meeting burdening people with an ever-increasing list of critical actions. Particularly if you are having frequent meetings to ensure that appropriate (or merely demanded) updates can be passed to senior management or media relations,† then your meeting cycle may be tighter than any reasonable (or, if you are really unlucky) rational cycle of activities.

Where an incident is relatively stable or where the activities in progress are likely to take time to do correctly,‡ it may be worth reducing the planned frequency of meetings or, where this is politically unacceptable, simply checking whether there have been any material changes in the situation. The art of expectancy management, covered in Chapter 16, is an important consideration here.

Activity merely for activity's sake is, at best, nugatory and will usually distract resource that could be resting, changing shift or moving between home and work. However, if you feel that there are appropriate activities that should be undertaken, do not let the guidance above push you towards procrastination.

---

* Although, even amongst the geekiest, incident responders rarely have as terrible hair as media pundits and second-string politicians.

† The two most common culprits, there are others.

‡ Implementing software fixes, replacing hardware, recovery from offline backups, as examples.

Investigation Activities

Depending on the sort of incident you are investigating and the current context, there is an enormous range of individual investigations activities that you might be tasking your team with. It would not be reasonable to give even the most partial list, as the circumstances of readers' technology platforms, resources and experience will vary hugely, even assuming similar incident types.

Categories of Activity

However, activities can be split into a few basic types:

- Confirmatory
- Preparatory
- Exploratory
- Advisory
- Housekeeping

For some of these activities, you will be able to be quite prescriptive, for example "Get a copy of Dr. X's email account from the latest backup using our established call-out procedure for the Messaging 3rd Level Support Team." For others, you are going to have to rely on the experience and professionalism of your team.* This requires you to know them, their strengths and their weaknesses, really quite well in order to assign rationally achievable tasks.

Confirmatory Activities   Where you have information but are not certain of its provenance or its accuracy, you may need to do some more in depth investigation in order to confirm it or to get additional details. This is a particularly important when you are considering resurrecting a closed incident as you need to be sure that the new information isn't just late arriving material from the previous incarnation. This is a particular problem with emails, as mass email waves from fraudsters will often result in stragglers being reported with extensive delays in transmission – several days is common.

---

* e.g. "See if you can recover any emails relating to X from the available backups." You'll notice that this is a much less bound task, in all areas of freedom, than the previous one. "Available backups" as opposed to "the latest functional backup" is clearly significantly more extensive.

Preparatory Activities   As the name suggests, any activities which are necessary to prepare the ground for subsequent work. This could include:

- Withdrawal of backup tapes from off-site storage.
- Restoration of backups onto an investigations server.*
- Obtaining privileged accounts for a system under investigation.
- Forensic first responder and imaging.

Exploratory Activities   This is the area most people would understand by "investigations":

- Searching for data sources, whether within your infrastructure, on partner systems or on the internet.
- Collecting the data – this is sometimes a technical exercise for the investigations team but more often involves finding somebody with existing legitimate privileges and persuading them to package it up appropriately and send it to you.†
- Processing collected data to make it readable – either for your tools or by your team. This can involve complex processes such as decrypting drive images.
- Sifting data for relevance, hoping to uncover useful information.
- Initial analysis of that information:

  - Is this completely new or is it supplementary to existing information?
  - Does it support or contradict the current understanding?
  - Does it indicate a possible increase or decrease in the priority of the incident?
  - Does it show that there is a new impact or does it modify your understanding of an existing impact? This may change the categorisation of an incident but, much more importantly, might affect the business requirements of the incident response.

---

* As opposed to onto a live or replacement server, which would be a restoration/ recovery action.
† This is just as true if it is a member of a technical support team within your own organization as for the manager of a system halfway around the world that has been hacked by fraudsters and is running a not-quite-accurate copy of your customer-facing website.

It can also cover research activities, for example:

- Into the existence or significance of vulnerabilities.
- Conducting penetration tests against representative laboratory systems.
- Even running malware in a simulated environment to determine the locations of bot control servers or data exfiltration locations.

Advisory Activities   This works both ways. Sometimes you are advising people on the incident and what they might do about it; it may have impacted on the service you are providing for your customers, or you may be talking to your internal media, customer or regulatory relations team, ensuring that the statement they are preparing is neither technically misleading nor specifically inaccurate.

On the other hand, you may be getting advice from other specialists. These can be technical – your ISP, the vendors of software affected by the attack, or of your security devices. Human resources teams, lawyers and law enforcement can all provide useful advice in appropriate circumstances.

Housekeeping   Where the investigation is progressing reasonably and, as previously discussed, there are no pressing new activities to occupy your team, it is well worth considering "tidying things up a bit, in advance." This can cover a wide range of support activities, all aimed at propping up the investigation and ensuring that when you do need to up the work-rate again, people are ready to meet the demands.

- *Making certain that evidential integrity is maintained*: This can include the making of contemporaneous notes where it hasn't been practical to take them at the time of the activity or putting components in to fresh evidence bags and returning them to secure storage.
- *It can involve technical changes*: Disabling high privilege accounts that are not currently required, undoing temporary bodges where there is now a more considered fix in place or returning to pool systems that have been used for investigatory restores.
- *Personnel need maintenance too*: Sending somebody out to the local takeaway or just the decent coffee shop around the corner. Sending people home, if you can, even if you expect them to be back working on the incident once they are there. Releasing people, if it is temporarily quiet, for rest periods.

The Theory of Events (and Why There Shouldn't Be Just One!)   Sometimes, it is very obvious what has happened. Sometimes, it only seems that way. Much of the time, at the start of any incident, you may know at least some of the impacts of the incident but the "what" and the "why" may be a complete mystery.

As the investigation progresses, you will begin to build up what is properly known as a "Theory of Events." There are a couple of important things to ensure you remember. At least in the initial stages, any ToE is best described as an "educated guess," so you need to ensure that you don't become too wedded to it as "the truth." The second issue is more subtle and is related to the concept of "Prosecution Capture."*

Where a team has developed a ToE which is both credible and robust to the existing evidence, people will have an unfortunate tendency to look for evidence either directly supporting it or weighing against any alternatives.[†] This is not quite as blatant as ignoring contradictory information, but it is a bias in the search for or through the data that skews what is then presented to a decision maker or equivalent forum.

It is therefore well worth identifying a number of different, complementary ToEs and maintaining at least a couple of non-preferred options in the back of your mind throughout the investigations process. It is also, where worth formulating an appropriate null hypothesis – "there is nothing malicious occurring" or "there is no new incident."

Restorative Activities

Although it does occasionally happen otherwise,[‡] most incidents will involve some degree of restorative activity. Usually, this will not be the direct responsibility of the incident manager (although they may also be responsible for this in another hat), but will usually be the responsibility of one or more ICT teams.

---

* Where the various entities in a criminal prosecution get so caught up in the social need to punish the perpetrator of some hideous wrongdoing that they develop a form of group-think and ignore the fact that the arrested or accused person may not actually be that criminal.

[†] An example may be the extreme cultural reluctance of some organizations to consider wrongdoing by employees as opposed to partners, customers or third parties.

[‡] Forensics investigations on an end-user device, for example.

Your primary role will usually be to de-conflict these activities from the others underway and to ensure that appropriate reports on issues with the activities are included in incident progress updates.

Notification and Reporting

This is a complex area, deserving of a chapter of its own. Which, in the way of these things, you can find at Chapter 16.

Suffice it to say at this point, that there will be a range of people interested in the occurrence or progress of your incident as well as a number of people or organization s who you are required, legally, contractually, or by internal procedures, to inform.

Monitor and Review

Having completed some tasks or task elements, reported to management and made sure that the team are surviving, it is important to review both the progress on the existing tasks and whether there is a need to modify current or planned activities to take note of new information or changes in the business requirements.

Depending on the speed that the incident is moving, you will have a lot of these meetings therefore it is important that the meetings themselves take the minimum amount of effort away from the investigative (and recovery) tasks. Earlier meetings may have to be longer, as there is more likely to be a greater change in the information available since the previous meeting so that it is essential that people are released as soon as practical.

If you have small teams working on particular tasks, it is not always necessary to have all of the team members at the progress meeting, although, where you are in a degree of doubt about the best method of progressing the incident, you run the risk of excluding potential sources of ideas.

When to Break Out?

One problem with any cyclical model is escaping from it. In fact, many of them (such as the Deming cycle – Plan, Do, Check, Act) are deliberately designed as such a perpetual trap.

Clearly, if new or changing information is arriving, the incident still needs to be treated as within the investigations cycle, as modifications to the business requirements, your desired end state and the appropriate activities to reach that state may also need to change in response.

In the case of incidents, your first indication is likely to be a drop in the frequency with which you need to hold the progress meetings – the cycle will slow and the number of housekeeping activities will generally rise.

"Special handling" incidents of all types will usually remain within the investigations cycle for considerably longer, due to the nature of the evidence gathering and processing required before critical treatment decisions will be made (usually not by the incident manager).

It is not always necessary for all activities to be complete before closing the incident, but depending on the type of incident and the precise types of authority held by the incident team, some activities, particularly exploratory,* will need to be managed within the incident context. Other activities, including recovery tasks, particularly those which are conducted under the authority of other teams, may continue once you have closed the incident.

If the incident has been lengthy, it is usually reasonable to call a break to allow people to have a rest and be able to look more dispassionately at the situation before formal closure. This also, especially in the case of external attacks, gives a chance for any recurrence of the attack to be detected before the team is disbanded.

In the end, the decision has to be one for the incident manager, especially as they will be the person faced with restarting the incident if they take the decision too early and potentially without the resources they are currently allocated. It is very much a matter of experience and it is not inappropriate for a less experienced manager to delay formal closure until they are fully convinced that the team are no longer required.

Keeping Control of Your Investigation

Revealing the Case Studies

As Amber Inc. is a large company it is more likely that incidents have greater complexity than might be expected with a smaller. There may

---

* Because of the use of privileges and the potential for invasions of both privacy and corporate confidentiality.

also be different areas of the business that need to be involved in the process of investigating and restoring "normal working." For example, communication with the media or customers in a company of this size is likely to be controlled through the PR department. It would be their job to both respond to queries from the press and to provide briefing information for external facing help desks who would be expected to support customers through any impact that the incident might have on them. In an organization of this size, there may also be a number of different people or teams who expect to be regularly briefed. When the incident is still in the investigation phase, that can be frustrating both for those who are communicated with the interested parties and those who have to brief them; as there may be little new information to divulge.

It is also important to acknowledge that there may be internal politics, even at the active stage, that is preparing ensuring that as little blame as possible becomes attached to them personally, or their team. However, expectancy management, both the expectation of a solution to the issue or a restoration of the services, can be put in place early. A wise head of IR, for example, does not estimate recovery until they have as full a picture of the scope of the issue as possible. If they are lucky an early promise of time to recovery might be delivered, but if it can't be the frustration and disappointment is compounded.

Jade Ltd. has a two-fold problem in this cyclical phase of investigation. Firstly, the IM team has very little experience in dealing with such problems, and therefore, it is more likely that finding a route cause will take longer or be side tracked by false trails and possible diagnosis. Also, they are somewhat at the mercy of their ISP data centre, which means they may be affected by incidents that are at the centre over which they have no control. However, that does not mean that they should not have processes in place to investigate incidents. Before it can be established where the problem lies and to what extent Jade Ltd.'s IM team can take any action to restore, the incident needs to be understood; it's origin effects and any action, whether that is to mitigate or to deal with the problem directly. Exactly the same methodology as demonstrated above can help Jade Ltd. and its staff both understand the nature of the problem and reduce the risk from a repeat, but also see how the impact of future situations can be mitigated in future.

It is also essential that the IM team are familiar with the contracted agreement between the organization and the data centre, especially with regard to agreed restoration priorities. As Jade Ltd. is a small company, the data centre may not have them as a top priority for restoration. In this case, Jade Ltd. has to have contingency plans to maintain as much of the normal business processes as possible.

Annex A: Managing the Incident Meeting

Hopefully, you are an experienced enough manager (or, indeed, executive) to have no problem in running a meeting. You will be aware that preparation is often the key to a good meeting – a proper agenda,* ensuring everybody has pre-read discussion documents and ensuring proper time-keeping. Even using practices such as the "stand-up" to keep meetings short.

However, in many incident response scenarios, you will not have the advantages of preparation, you probably will not have chance to circulate documents prior to the meeting,† and you probably won't have a meeting secretary.

A Short Meeting

In the early stages of any incident, the primary object is to get everybody back to working on the incident, while allowing you to take proper notice of any changes in the business requirement, the circumstances of the incident or the resources available.

Firstly, make sure that any documentation produced is discussed prior to the meeting so that relevant options, or, if it is within your comfort zone, your fait accompli, can be presented.

The meeting should follow something like this basic agenda:

- Does anybody‡ have new information which suggests we may be doing the wrong things?

---

* Flexible enough, and properly amended and announced that "any other (competent) business" does not become the majority of the meeting.
† And everybody, except audit, if you have been forced to let them in, will have been too busy to give them more than a cursory glance.
‡ It is often useful to make it compulsory for all attendees to contribute at this point. Especially if you have relatively inexperienced team members, this is a useful tool to make sure they feel that they are allowed to contribute.

- An update, from you, on any direction from higher management on the business requirements or reports down from higher level meetings.
- Very brief updates on current actions – these should be limited to:
  - Complete
  - Ongoing according to plan
  - Ongoing but delayed
  - Stalled
  - Not yet started
- Lead a review of any new actions required and any reprioritisation of existing actions.
- Assignment of resources to the actions.
- Time of next meeting.

If You Have the Time

Generally, there is a useful structure to the meeting and some of it is very similar:

1. Is there anything urgent somebody needs to bring up that might mean the meeting should be postponed or repurposed to deal with it?
2. Status on progress on actions from the last meeting. Make this very brief to start with, using something similar to the short meeting report. Where any aspect of this is a surprise or of concern to you, you can then go back to the teams or individuals for a more detailed report.
3. *New information*: This is the meat of the meeting. Is there any new information, as a result of team activities or from elsewhere, that might change your perception of the situation? If the information is unclear or from a source of dubious reliability, but would be material to your understanding of the incident if correct, then you have some confirmatory activities for somebody to undertake.
4. *New direction or advice*: Changes in business requirements or advice from legal or other sources will affect your actions.
5. *New actions or proposed modifications to existing actions*: This should be a bit of a round-table exercise, allowing suggestions

from all present, if you have time but culminating in the incident manager proposing a course of action and having this approved by the senior business representative.

6. *Allocation of actions*: Depending on how radical the changes agreed were, this may require re-tasking of teams. Where people do not have any obvious actions assignable – do they have secondary skills which could assist another team or aspect of the investigation?

7. That would normally conclude the formal meeting – although "any other business" will usually be called, the team should be encourage to bring up any aspects in the relevant main section.

8. Longer reports can now be taken with only the relevant people attending and most away back at work. If necessary, critical aspects can be briefed in to, or the reports made available prior to, the next meeting.

Annex B: Sensibly Setting Tasks

Try to Be SMART

When you are setting tasks of whichever type, it is useful to remember, if not to be bound by, the "SMART Objectives criteria."*

- Specific[†] – people are going to be tired and stressed. The more guidance you can give them when setting the task, the better they are likely to achieve it.[‡]

---

[*] If this particular bit of management speak has eluded you, then the Wikipedia page "SMART criteria" is a very good primer. Please note, for the more technical reader, that I am not, in any way, referring to "Self-Monitoring, Analysis, and Reporting Technology" as available on some hard disk drives near you. Other storage devices, as well as other management fads, are available!

[†] Or "Simple." Quite a lot of the time, your team will be having to liaise with people out with the incident management sphere so ensuring that any task can be described in, ideally, simple English or, if absolutely necessary, common IT jargon is vital. Where needed, split a task into simpler elements – you can still give these all to the same person but it also helps with the rest of our criteria.

[‡] Although this does need to be balanced against being patronizing to the more experienced of your team. In that case, you might set them the task in general terms and then get them to split it for you in to simpler component task elements, either as part of the meeting or immediately afterwards (but still forming part of the meeting record.)

- "Who," You need to detail off the resources that you are employing on this task – personnel and technical.
- They need to know what you intend them to achieve.*
- Usually, if your team are reasonably experienced, the "why" element will either be blatantly obvious or generally accepted – you have an incident ongoing, after all – although you may need to give guidance to newer team members or secondees. You need to be more careful here when you are undertaking invasive investigations that will compromise peoples' privacy – the "why" may need to formally refer to the detailed justification for the privacy breach.
- "When," when it isn't immediately (and it often is), needs to be both spelt out and, for purposes of expectancy management (theirs, yours and your managements), recorded. Often you will have activities that will need to wait until the start of working hours – either in your location or if you need to contact, say, a hosting company or a registrar in a foreign location.
- "Where," where it isn't obvious, may also need to be detailed. Remember that people may not be operating at their best and, provided you can keep it from becoming personal,† specific is better than vague. In the incident management context, one vital aspect of "where" are contact details, both for the team and for those they will be liaising or working with.
- *Measurable*: The team (and you) need to have a fairly clear idea what success looks like for each task or element thereof. That way, they know when they can stop and return to being taskable resource for you for the next part of the job.
- *Achievable (also "realistic," although that is sometimes used below)*: Simply enough – you need to ensure that not only is what you

---

* This is, of course, particularly important if you are sending somebody to the coffee shop!

† If you feel you need to be explicit, yet you feel this may be taken badly, perhaps you can deflect it towards yourself. Remind people that you have to report upwards and that you need to ensure your reports are clear on current activities. You may have better or, at least, more appropriate ideas.

- Relevant – to the overall achievement of one or more of the business requirements. Admittedly, you may find yourself needing to undertake some activities to appease management (who do have their fads and foibles) but try to leave those, if you can, until a relatively quiet time in the overall cycle.*
- *Time-Bound*: Regardless of whether the task is immediate or, for some reason delayed, it should be something that can be significantly progressed, if not completed, in a small multiple of the time interval between your progress review meetings.† Again, where this is impractical (a complex task may actually be best handled by one person or a small team, who are given a high degree of freedom of action), split or get them to split, the task into elements with a shorter time to fruition.

---

* Cynically, if they really are demanding nugatory effort and cannot be deflected, you could always employ the tactic made infamous by Sir Robert Armstrong, then the British Cabinet Secretary and now Baron Armstrong of Ilminster and be "economical with the truth." That may, of course, not be a wise or (career) safe course of action.

† We've already mentioned Matthew's phone destroying weekend incident. One of the more irritating aspects was that formal meetings were held every hour and normally lasted for about 55 minutes. This gave time for a quick trip to the loo and to grab a cup of tea (caffeine being essential in these circumstances and Matthew being allergic to coffee). Not a lot of time to progress any actions and, really, not enough time to get reports from his team on what and how they were doing.

9

ROLES AND RESPONSIBILITIES

On the sea there is a tradition older even than the traditions of the country itself and wiser in its age than this new custom. It is the tradition that with responsibility goes authority and with them accountability.

... for men will not long trust leaders who feel themselves beyond accountability for what they do.

... And when men lose confidence and trust in those who lead, order disintegrates into chaos and purposeful ships into uncontrollable derelicts.

"On The Collision of Wasp and Hobson"
Wall Street Journal, Editorial
14 May 1952

Information in this chapter:

- The incident manager
- Separation of duties: management, reporting and operations
- Dedicated IM staff
- Support staff and communications
- Creating an effective incident management team

Introduction

One of the most important aspects to get clear even if you cannot manage to get it right, whatever that happens to be for your organization, is the allocation of responsibilities and if that can be managed, the appropriate authorities necessary to meet those (and, if not, the 24 × 7 contact numbers for the people who actually do have the authority). This will then allow you to construct a number of incident management roles and to allocate those within your organization, whether you are talking about dedicated staff, temporary secondees from other areas of the organization, or external suppliers or contractors.

Without this structure, even competent teams can flounder in a sea of competing priorities, unavailability of specialist advice, and even an active refusal to co-operate.

The Incident Manager

The incident manager is, reasonably obviously, one of if not the most vital role in an incident response team. Unfortunately, it is quite a hard one to fill, and we'll look at recruitment and selection later. It is normally preferable, unless you are in a formal "Security Operations Centre" context with planned and practised shift changes (and sometimes even then) for the same individual to remain as the manager throughout an incident.

It is essential that the incident manager has appropriate authority to deal with all aspects of the incident – including out of hours. This needs to include authority to call out supporting members of staff and contractors, a degree of spending authority, and authority to require IT and similar support functions to take necessary investigative and corrective actions.

Where it is not appropriate within the organizational context to grant this authority,* and that will depend on the culture of the organization, the seniority of the individual manager and the maturity of the Incident Management process in the eyes of executive management, they need real-time access to the people with that authority. In a limited number of cases, a post-hoc approvals process may be appropriate, such as for expenditure above a certain limit, although this is generally ineffective except in smaller organizations.

---

* You would not necessarily expect, as an example, the incident manager to have individual authority to approve changes to business critical live systems in a large financial organization, but then, they need the authority to call a meeting of the "Emergency Change Board" or similar.

The Lead Investigator

Unless your response team is particularly small,* it will usually be necessary for somebody to be appointed the lead investigator. They would, like the incident manager, generally expect to stay with the incident from start to finish. This is not a seniority role but a co-ordinating one, acting as a deputy to the incident manager, especially when they are not able to attend meetings or brief other technical staff (often because they are, themselves, reporting up the hierarchy.)

Separation of Duties

The incident manager has three main roles. They are primarily there to ensure that the response team keep sight of the organization's goals in the overall response and to ensure that appropriate resources are made available to allow the activities to continue efficiently. In most circumstances, they will also be the person to keep appropriate management informed of the progress (or lack thereof) in the response. This actually fills a dual role – often the most useful thing they are doing here is preventing, particularly in serious incidents, executives micro-managing the incident response and, particularly, from having "good ideas."†

Investigation Technicians

These are the trained and experienced IM staff. They will almost always have an IT and often an IS background and will need training in the rules of evidence as well as being provided with small amounts of seizure equipment and other tools.

Where your organization is quite widely dispersed but your professional incident team is in central locations, it will often be quite sensible to train up what are normally referred to as "forensic first

---

* Remember that even large companies have small incidents. Most of the incidents Matthew has dealt with, in sheer numerical terms, were dealt with by the two on-call people. Often, frankly, with minimal involvement from one or the other of even those.

† Internal audit and finance are particularly prone to this.

responders." This can be of particular value where you are crossing significant jurisdictional boundaries as far as the admissibility aspects of the rules of evidence are concerned. These will be trusted people – often IT junior management, local security operations staff or even internal audit – whose role is not necessarily to conduct any investigations activities themselves, but to seize and preserve evidential material either for the arrival on site of your investigators or to courier the material to the appropriate central team.

Technical and Support Staff

This will depend very much on the nature of your organization, your ICT infrastructure and the amount of contracting and outsourcing you undertake. You will clearly need to involve networking experts, your security operations team and your internal and customer support helpdesks. However, outside of the technical realm, you are also going to need to ensure that you have appropriate contacts in:

- The internal fraud investigations function, if such exists.
- Human Resources, particularly the disciplinary experts.
- Legal – including an access route for external legal advisors, if these are appointed rather than obtained in an ad hoc manner.
- Internal Audit – investigations may uncover aspects of organizational failure or behaviour that require longer-term monitoring and, possibly, formal reporting. This is, from hard-gained experience, best left to the experts.
- Media and Customer Relations – you are unlikely to want to talk to the press or to customers, largely because you are likely to be much too busy. However, you also need to ensure that, in any incident, false information is not provided, so you will need not just the contacts but to understand what they will require and how they think so that you can provide them with the appropriate information to allow them to construct truthful* briefings.

---

* "Truthful" and "informative" are wholly different. "We are investigating the allegations and will provide further information once we have a proper understanding of the situation," is an ideal statement in the early stages of a public incident – even if you already have a fairly good idea what might have been going on.

- Purchasing – your incident team will need specialist equipment and may also want to buy IT outside of the normal channels.* Specific incidents may involve an urgent requirement for significant amounts of hard disks and backup tapes, for example, or specialist photography printing services.

External Contractors

You will also need contacts within your existing external suppliers and probably some investigations specific contractors.

Your corporate ISP and datacentre providers and any off-site backup provider are essential contacts and will probably need to be brought in to your IM exercises because of the wide range of issues that they may be involved in. If you outsource security or network monitoring or your WAN provision, these will also be vital resources to you, both as providers of information and also of specialist technical expertise.

Your IT and communications vendors are also critical and you will need to work with the account managers in case there is an issue that requires investigation or addressing at the infrastructure level – you might be unlucky enough to be one of the early victims of a so-called "zero-day" attack or malware infection. No matter how capable your team, you are almost certainly going to have to rely on external support for the full and final restoration of services.

Unless you are creating your own forensics services team, you will want call-off access to forensics support.

Law Enforcement

Matthew, working for a large organization, found it very important to establish friendly relations with the local and national electronic crime investigations units. Even if you don't expect that you will be in a position to report much criminal activity (and the amount of hacker attacks and malware infections prevalent in the general environment means that law enforcement do have to be very selective in the cases they follow up on), the time may come when you do need, or even are legally required, to make a report.

---

* Forensics workstations which require to be permanently connected to the corporate LAN and are managed by your first level helpdesk are and so are not necessarily ideal, especially if you are investigating your first level helpdesk team.

At this point, it is vital both that you understand what information they will want – which may be very different to the information you would provide to your executive management, legal or HR functions – and what level of access they will require. In an ideal case, they may be happy to allow you to continue with your investigations and simply take the evidence and reports that you would collect and provide. In other cases, and you will want to know what these are, they will want to take immediate control.

Where law enforcement is willing to let you continue will vary widely between jurisdictions, normally they are significantly over-worked and white collar or electronic crime are rarely political or prosecution priorities, so they will welcome your help. However, this will vary.

Historically, in the United Kingdom, it was very difficult for non-police (or not formally contracted to the police) investigators to work on suspected paedophile imagery cases. The introduction of the Sexual Offences Act 2003 provided an additional statutory defence for possession of image in Section 43 for corporate investigators pursuing an investigation. Matthew's central team spanned England, where the Act applies, and Scotland, where it does not. Therefore, there had to be a split in process – any investigations in Scotland still required immediate reporting to the police, whereas, in England, after discussion with the main police computer crime and child protection units, the initial review could be conducted internally and then reported – with an indication for the police as to whether there was sufficient evidence to justify a police investigation.

Creating an Effective Team

At this point, you might be forgiven for thinking that, particularly for a small organization, that this is incredibly complex and expensive to do. However, the key elements that are required to respond to an incident could well be available from within the existing staff. If the requirement is new then building from within and seeing how that works with the incidents that occur with determinedly effective post incident reviews* can go a long way to moulding an effective team, whatever the size and demands.

---

* As opposed to those focused on political promotion or protection.

Revealing the Case Studies

Amber Inc.

With a larger resource pool, Amber Inc. should have fewer problems staffing a roster, particularly with a number of specialist security staff working for the IS manager. However, this greater profusion of people – and many IT staff find both security and, particularly, incident response quite fascinating – will lead to a significant selection and training burden, which is a difficult thing for a new team* that has to prove itself operational quite quickly to manage.

Also, within a larger organization, there may be the ability to manage authority more effectively. This does depend, to a great extent on organizational culture – but for the purposes of our examples, let us assume that Amber's culture allows the delegation of both authority over both operations and expenditure.

It might have been expected that an organization such as this would already have an established security incident response team, but actually many organizations operate with their existing IT department and help desk taking the strain. There are a number of reasons why this is an unhelpful approach in the long term.

- IT teams are unlikely to have the range of expertise required to handle incidents of the sort that modern business encounters, for example, HR, appropriate legal and forensic recovery and analysis.
- IT teams are busy enough dealing with keeping the system running.
- Not all incidents have IT causes or solutions.
- Budget for incident response type operations will come out of the normal budget, not recognised and funded separately.

Jade Ltd.

Jade Ltd. is just large enough to have a formal on-call team. At the moment, the security manager, the IT manager and his deputy will

---

* To be honest, selection of suitable staff is a major headache for even a well-established team. Training is less of a problem, once you have identified suitable basic providers and an on-the-job training package. Both will be covered in later chapters.

form the incident management rota, with the three remaining security staff forming the lead technician rota.

A team of four people is realistically the minimum needed for a formal rota system when you allow for illness, holidays and other absence from work such as residential training courses. So, there is clearly going to need to be cover cross-roster or from other areas. Goodwill can wear out quite quickly with over-work, especially as the day job still needs to be done

Of significant interest is going to be how they ensure that appropriate authority is delegated. Only the IT manager is senior enough to have significant delegated authority in his normal role and he is usually constrained to acting through programme boards or the change or emergency change boards. Neither the IS manager nor the deputy IT manager have financial authority or the ability to commit Jade Ltd. contractually.

10
POLICIES AND DOCUMENTATION

A Vogon wouldn't even lift a finger to save their own grandmothers from the Ravenous Bugblatter Beast of Traal without an order, signed in triplicate, sent in, sent back, queried, lost, found, subjected to public enquiry, lost again, and finally buried in soft peat for three months and recycled as firelighters.

Douglas Adams
Hitchhikers Guide to the Galaxy (1979)

Information in this chapter:

- What is the minimum necessary?
- Administrative requirements of successful IM
- Importance of post incident policy review and possible amendment
- Regulatory requirements for appropriate documentation

Introduction

Policies and documentation are a necessary evil. If there is too much, it is unlikely to be used properly or even read by the people who need to. If this means that processes are not properly followed then there can be legal, contractual or regulatory repercussions, even if the incident appears to have been handled properly.

However, if there is a lack of guidance or the documentation is insufficiently clear, then there is an equivalent risk of mismanagement or omission of critical elements of the response.

The level of documentation appropriate to your organization will depend on your culture, level of experience of incident managements and your regulatory environment. This chapter intends to provide an indicative minimum level of documentation and to indicate where additional material may be appropriate.

Formal Documentation

If you are within an ISO27001, PCI-DSS or (depending on your nationality) Government Information Security compliant organization, you will be required to have suitable documentation for your incident management organization. Although there is a reasonable degree of guidance in the relevant documentation, it is rarely comprehensive and it often omits some of the key organizational decisions that are essential to be laid out well before you need them in the incident.

Minimum Requirements

Documentation Levels

The important thing with documentation is to keep it useable. Therefore, it needs to be available when people need it, easy to find information in it, and as clear and concise as possible. You also need to remember that, especially if you are fortunate enough to be part of an organization that does not have very many security incidents, people will be referring to an unfamiliar document quite possibly in the early hours of the morning, having just had an unwelcome wake-up call.

Key Points

Regardless of exactly:

- *Policy*: People need to know what the executive direction and the default business requirements are.
- *Organization*: Who is minding the shop, who will get involved when something kicks off and who needs to make themselves available in case they are required.
- *Authority*: Who is in charge and what power do they have, especially if, as incident manager, they have authority additional to that from their day job. Additionally, who do they need to contact if they have exceeded that authority or urgently need to?

- *Process*: What is the basic process for incident management? Are there any variants (i.e. contractual or regulatory requirements for key customers)?
- *Procedures*: If you have developed standardised procedures for any specific incident type, these need to be included.
- *Contact Details*: For incident team members, key internal staff and relevant partners and other external agencies. Possibly for key customers as well.
- Checklists.

Many of these have been covered in detail in previous chapters or will be covered shortly.

Issuing Documentation

Generally, incident management documentation will either be arranged in a single handbook or in a tiered set of policy, process and procedure books.

Please remember, even in these days of e-offices and intranets, that the incident you are dealing with may have taken down your internal communications, so you will need backup copies. If you have gone for intranet issue of HTML or linked PDF books, or anything similar, either provide emergency paper copies, with the requirement to keep those up to date, or you may consider providing, off-line copies using e-readers or tablet* devices and ensure that these are available to, and downloaded by, key participants (this could be checked on your regular business continuity exercises – you do have these, don't you?)

Policy

As discussed earlier, the primary purpose of incident response is to support the business. Although specific incidents, in their own context, will generate quite different operational requirements, businesses will

---

* Depending on the sensitivity of your documentation, you may need to provide these devices or it may be reasonable to allow people to use their personal devices. If you do allow use of personal equipment, it is important to make sure that no sensitive information regarding individual incidents is retained on the devices.

generally have an overriding set of corporate requirements which should be laid out in advance.

For example:

- A business where most of its custom is online is likely to have availability, therefore service restoration, as the core requirement in all, barring the most extreme circumstances.
- Many businesses will be operating within a regulatory context. Even if the regulator has not laid down formal requirements or systems for incident response, ensuring that the incident is managed in a satisfactory way from the regulator's viewpoint will be essential, even if that means compromising some of the other business requirements.
- Personal privacy is acquiring greater social importance and legal recognition. If a personal data breach has occurred, or is alleged to have occurred, then there may be significant requirements or restrictions on the activities you might undertake.
- Different companies have very different attitudes to both internal discipline and to involving law enforcement. Knowing what the default corporate stance is and who has the authority to vary that is vital. Especially during detailed technical investigations, knowing that there is a wish to produce admissible evidence in a subsequent court case can restrict your flexibility in both what activities may be appropriate and what tools you might use to conduct them.

Accordingly, there needs to be some clear policy direction to incident responders on the executives' expectations and priorities during an incident. This document should be relatively brief and contain something along the lines of the following sections.

Executive Commitment

We suspect that this meme is repeated by every specialist area, but that doesn't make it untrue.

Overt and personal commitment by the executive and, ideally, nomination of a member of the executive to be accountable for security incident management helps to make the case to the business that your requirements are of at least a similar scale of importance as theirs. It is perhaps easiest to demonstrate the importance of this in terms of the repercussion for the lack of executive commitment. There may be a situation where an executive pressures incident staff to circumvent formal practice agreed in policy and procedure. If they are not willing to present a rational justification that can be recorded as part of the documentation, then the overall stress on staff increases and the effectiveness of incident handling is likely to decrease both in short and medium term.

Core Direction and Principles

There should be a brief statement of the executives' baseline requirements for any incident.

This should cover the corporate requirements discussed above and include reporting chains and frequencies and cover the interaction between IT operational incidents (e.g. ITIL or ISO20000 systems), security incidents and BC/DR teams.

Organization and Authority

It is essential that there is a clear statement, especially governing an increases in delegated authority that occur during incident response, approved by the top executive level in the company.

The composition of the incident management team needs to be stated – particularly, who is in charge and who must be involved.

Precise levels of authority available to the duty incident response team, individually or collectively, need to be stated, as does the process for gaining any authority in excess of that granted as of right.

Law Enforcement, Regulators, Media and Customers

Going outside the organization, except to close partners, is likely to be contentious. The executive management needs to lay down their requirements for approval or otherwise before contact is made externally, particularly with those organizations or groups where there could be a significant risk of business or reputational damage.

It is usually also helpful to detail who, and under what circumstance, is permitted to make contact.[*]

Process

The bulk of the documentation is likely to be in your process documentation. This will contain details on timelines, categorisation and the expected workflow and reporting, as have been covered in the previous chapters.

The format and details will very much depend on your organizational culture. However, it is essential to have clear to follow guidelines and a number of checklists to ensure that inexperienced incident managers are provided with sufficient information in a suitable format to ensure that no critical actions, reports or checkpoints are missed.

Work Instructions

As the organization learns from various incidents, it may be possible to develop detailed work instructions for dealing with specific incident types.

Because incidents, even of similar type, tend to vary widely (otherwise, they are likely to be closer to a "security issue" rather than an incident), you should ensure that all incident response staff are aware that the work instructions are indicative rather than prescriptive.[†]

It may be most appropriate to include work instructions in a checklist rather than prose format.

Incident Administration

During the conduct of an incident, it will be necessary to record a number of items, particularly those relevant to key decisions taken. If

---

[*] Matthew's opinion, for what it is worth, is that the only one of the organizations named in the subsection title that the incident response team have any business talking to are law enforcement. The rest are best left to the specialists in that particular area.

[†] Where work instructions contain legal or regulatory mandatory steps or detailed technical instructions, this should be made clear.

it is possible, and especially if it is likely, that an incident will result in legal action, significantly more detailed notes will be required. Further details are in Chapter 12.

Revealing the Case Studies

Amber Inc.

Amber Inc. are an international company and so care must be taken to ensure polices and documentation are consistent with any legal or regulatory requirements in the different countries and are reviewed on a regular basis. Legal requirements can change, especially in reaction to a change in the threat landscape. It is easy for such change, especially if it is restricted to just one country, to be overlooked, and therefore, not revised in line with the change. This could lead to significant financial and reputational damage to the organization.

As will be discussed in more detail in Chapter 19, the review of an incident after closure can lead to recommendations and changes to the process of incident handling. Depending whether these are local or central there may be changes made at the local level and it is important that these are also noted by the central IR team as it may affect their support in future.

Working to carefully laid out policies and controls can be frustrating, indeed there may be different cultural reactions to such documentation which could lead to significant differences in implementation. Again, this is best controlled by central oversight by someone who has a good understanding of the cultural and legal environment in which the team is operating. In this situation, it may be more difficult to develop a suitable relationship with significant external bodies such as the police. This should not be overlooked however, as the peak of a significant incident is a bad time to find no point of contact with such bodies.

Jade Ltd.

Jade Ltd. is fundamentally a service provider and their customers are going to grow more fussy about security and business continuity in the next few years. It's therefore essential that appropriate records of incidents are kept as close to contemporaneously as possible. This will make complying with external audit requirements will take less time and stress, and it will give a good impression of an organization that takes the security of customer data seriously.

11

SELECTING, BUILDING AND MOTIVATING YOUR TEAM

Coming together is a beginning.
Keeping together is progress.
Working together is success.

Henry Ford

Information in this chapter:

- Team composition
- The pressures of incident response
- Who volunteers for IR work
- How to motivate IR team members
- Building the team
- The importance of trust and mutual assurance
- Understanding and responding to motivation

Introduction: What Have You Let Yourself in For?

People who have not managed a team that has out-of-hours incident response responsibilities may well underestimate the challenge involved in carrying out this task effectively. If that describes you, then you might start by considering what you feel are going to be your main challenges. Is it going to be the demands of the operational task or the management of the staff under your charge? In most cases, the answer will be more complex than a binary choice might suggest. It may be some of the task and some of the people. It may even be that you don't feel you know enough about the role to give an unequivocal answer.

Standard "9 to 5" management involves managing tasks and staff in carrying out those tasks. In many cases, that is a very challenging task in itself. However, incident response means that you will have to consider other factors such as preferences for availability; for example, some staff may not wish to work on their Sabbath or holy day. This sort of thing rarely affects standard working but will have an effect on rotas and even duty lengths, and there are many other similar considerations. It could be said that what is required are many of the same skills as any good manager, but also be more aware of what is going on with staff and operations, In the words of Sherlock Holmes: *"You see, but you do not observe. The distinction is clear."**

Forming an effective team requires skill in any circumstances. A fundamental reason for that is that a good team is a mix of different skills and personalities.

Team Composition

Before deciding on the people and skills you are going to need to comprise your IR team, there are a number of matters you need to establish:

- What capabilities are going to be required from the IR team?
- What is the budget?
- Do you have an internal applicant pool?
- What is the organizational attitude towards external recruitment?
- How will the balance work between the core team and those members of the wider team comprising of staff who are based in other teams but can be used from time to time?

There are lots of academic and more popular ideas for the different balance of characters that you need in a team – introvert types and initiators amongst others. The one I like best came out of the head of a colleague of mine when I lectured in management. As a management team, we would sometimes debate the various merits of team theories, but this one was always a favourite, as it was grounded in an example that was familiar and yet said a lot for character blend. Good teams

---

* Sherlock Holmes, *A Scandal in Bohemia*. Sir Arthur Conan Doyle, published in *The Strand Magazine* 1891.

have a similar collection of characters as the personalities in *Winnie the Pooh**:

> *Tigger*: There will often be a bouncy person. You will know them by their enthusiasm and their determination to see the positive side to situations. On the negative side, they will often not be circumspect or cynical enough and may miss things, but then that is why they are at their best in a team.
>
> *Rabbit*: There are a number of aspects to Rabbit. To start with, he has lots of friends and relations, this can be paralleled as the person in the team who knows everyone and knows who to talk to for specific help and is probably on first name terms with them. This character is also a precious, prickly and particular about how things are done. This can be really helpful – you certainly need a "Rabbit" to counter balance a "Tigger" who may act on their gut instinct.
>
> *Owl (or as he spells it, Wol)*: Owl is the one all the others defer to almost without question. He is a great one for being able to justify himself when questioned, but one of the jokes for the reader is that he is often wrong. If there is a person in the team who has a lot of knowledge this is a lesson learnt that others would never be afraid to question or drill down into their ideas. Nobody in an IR team, no matter how long in the tooth, should be given unquestioning deference.
>
> *Kanga*: This is the calm person who can stand in the middle of the chaos and deal with the issues in a clear way. They may not have all the best ideas but knows how to get it and who can do tasks best. This may be the manager, but not necessarily, I have known some very good "Tigger" bosses who just make sure they have a balanced team around them. In the original books of course, Kanga is the mother figure who cares and protects. That may be a role you need in the team, perhaps not one who 'mothers' in an overly protective way, maybe one who is just good at noticing when other team members are "off

---

* *Winnie the Pooh* by A. A. Milne.

their game," which may be because they are ill or an issue that requires management intervention.

Eeyore: Ah, well yes, there is no getting away from it, most teams have someone in them who has the depressive attitude, if only part of the time. Now the important point with Eeyore is that he is not stupid. Actually, he tries to teach Piglet his letters and is a sharp observer and appraiser of those around him. An Eeyore can be annoying, as can the others to be honest, but he is diligent and has a doggedly persistent attitude to problem solving. He may moan, but that is what personal headphones are for isn't it?

Piglet: Piglet is small and timid but loyal and brave (for his size). In many teams, this character may describe the new recruit with little experience, or it may be anyone who has ability but lacks confidence. There is nothing in the stories that suggests that he is without ability and that is an important point, but it is clear that he won't develop without being mentored and encouraged. This person may be eased into the team with care taken about responsibility, but care should be taken as they are a burden, to a certain extent, while they are still inexperienced.

The Aim of the Incident Response Team

Here, you have to be very honest. The composition and even the amount of investment, needed in a team that is being created principally as part of a compliance exercise is going to need different staffing that one created to focus on key or principle threats that have been identified as significant by the organization. These may require new staff or retraining to provide staff with specific skills such as forensic analysis.

Establishing the exact nature of the service your incident response team will provide is also important, as it allows other staff who may first encounter or be informed of a problem to know how they should respond themselves, what the processes are, in order for the IR team to deal with the task most effectively. The other factor that is important in establishing the IR team is to establish, and clearly communicate the sort of commitment that would be required by incident response staff. Would there need to be a willingness to work any time 24/7 or is it expected that response would normally be confined within standard working hours?

A Question of Budget

Budget in this context means in cash rather than time so, for example, there needs to be a decision made with regard to what technical kit will be required to support the team. There is, for example, no point in spending staffing budget on a forensic specialist and not have the budget to provide the equipment they need to carry out the task. The level of the budget can influence whether to develop internal candidates for the roles or bring in external experience. However, it should also be remembered that skills, especially those linked to technology, do require regular professional development courses and events to stay current and effective. A wise manager will make themselves familiar with the financial demands these are likely to make in advance. It may also be worth getting advice from experienced IR managers as to which events and courses are cost effective to attend, and which are just slickly promoted. Once the team gets going, you may not have time to do this so it is as well to invest the time early on.

Internal Applicant Pool

For various reasons, including budget and familiarity with organizational systems, it may be desired that a high proportion of the new team be drawn from reassigning staff or adding IR responsibilities to their job if the demands of the task are not thought to require their full time attention. Also, if a core of a new team comprised of people who know each other and perhaps have worked together, at least in a project work, that can save time and expense. However, it is possible that there may not be some skills that are not available from the existing internal pool, or there is just a need to consider both internal candidates and external ones. This discussion will need to involve the human resources department amongst others but requires a clear view of the role of the IR team.

Motivation of Applicants

It is worth asking yourself why someone would volunteer for a place on the IR team the answer to this will help you develop an appropriate approach to the management of the team. There are a range of answers, and very few of them would be wrong, but some would be more indicative of a probable short-term commitment than a longer one. For example, someone who has recently experienced a change in social circumstances, such as divorce or separation, may see IR work, especially if it involves a significant out of hours commitment, as filling a void. While that is fine, it is also possible that a couple of years down the line, things may change again as they form new relationships or find new pastimes. It is also possible that someone living alone for the first time in a while may underestimate the challenges of long, stressful hours without home support. However, someone who has previously worked in a situation where there is an element of out of hours or flexible working may find normal working hours restrictive and be keen to work in this way again.

Money is a powerful motivator. In these tricky economic times, extra salary to compensate for out-of-hours work can give staff a bit more economic comfort. In exchange, it would be. Where there is a strong financial incentive to work in the IR team, it can help the manager if they know which of the team have that as a central motivator. For example, this means that if there was an attempt, further down the line to restrict out of hour payment, the manager would have some insight into the impact on the team; for example, which members they would be most likely to leave, and can use the cost of replacement of that person in further discussions with those setting budgets.

The Pressures of Incident Response

This will again depend on the reason behind the creation of this team, but if we assume this is to be an active team with varied work inside and sometimes outside normal working hours, it is even more important that the team have respect and understanding for each other's skills. Even if the team is principally working in standard working day time, it is easy to underestimate the additional demands of varied and time critical demands for solutions can be. In those circumstances, team members can, and will, become tired and that can lead to the danger of poor perception of the comparative effort. This is bad enough in a normal working team with resentment and cooperation do not go well together. Where team work is happening under pressure potential interpersonal or skills based problems need to be identified early. Indeed, much of the skill of a manger of an IR team is in being particularly aware of issues approaching and having methods of dealing with those that are both fair and perceived as fair by the team.

The variety of the problems that will be presented to the IR team over time makes it most likely that mistakes will be made. For some people, especially those who have worked in larger, politicised, environments, taking a rational, problem solving attitude to mistakes can be very difficult. This is often because their experience is that having their name associated with even a relatively minor mistake may be perceived as career limiting. As will be discussed elsewhere, it is vital that areas of weakness both personally and procedurally are identified and solutions found. This requires trust and from that will come a higher probability of honesty from the team and better development. I am not saying that you should encourage mistakes, far from it. Having a situation where mistakes are openly discussed and solutions devised is not the same as saying that mistakes are acceptable, but it does make for better development of procedure, policy and process within the organization as a whole.

An important factor to consider when staffing an incident response team is that the requirements for staff to take time out from out-of-hours work. There may be many reasons for this including the arrival of a new baby in the family or a growing dependency of an older or infirm relative. Where a sabbatical from out-of-hours working by mutual agreement with the manager is reasonably common and accepted, staff can be more forthcoming in identifying a need or anticipated need before the stress of continuing without help can lead to a longer, or permanent, absence of a valued team member.

Revealing the Case Studies

Amber Inc.

The Amber Inc. Incident Response Team will be devised with careful reference to the requirements of their customers and ISO27001. This means that they need to be aware of their risks and their risk appetite and it will be that which drives the sort of skills and experience they will need to include. Good advice, whether internal or external, will be required in order to fulfil their requirements as quickly as possible. For example, there are significant differences between the established ISO 27001 and the 2013 version, and advice must be based on the newer version, even if customers have yet to make their own changes to the newer version. The penalty for not taking action to meet customer need quickly may be the loss of important customers, which may have a significant impact on profits.

A second issue may be that they are a multinational organization. Depending on time zones, this might make out-of-hours work more common as action is co-ordinated between different regions. The different areas of operation might also affect the culture within the different regions which could impact on how staff who might need to work with the core IR team could be selected and motivated. HR and other relevant staff may have useful input on how this can be done.

Jade Ltd.

It is clear that Jade Ltd. have quite an urgent need to create an IR team both because of the sensitivity of the information they handle and because customers reporting problems are going to expect remediating action to be taken. Because of their use of data centres, it is critical that the remit of the IR team be carefully devised in order to make best use of the IR function at the data centres.

It is clear that one of the core challenges for Jade Ltd.'s IR team is the lack of expertise currently available to them within the organization. It will therefore probably be necessary to organise training of staff quickly and effectively, and probably attempt to recruit someone with skill and experience of IR in a similar situation. Recruitment can be expensive so it is important that those devising the specification for the job have a good understanding of the sort of person that is desired, both in terms of their qualification and experience. Taking up references before the end of any probationary period will be vital to ensure they will bring to the team the required skills and expertise.

12

INFORMATION AND COMMUNICATIONS SYSTEMS

You ask me if I keep a notebook to record my great ideas. I've only had one.

Albert Einstein

Information in this chapter:

- Introduction
- Record keeping
- System requirements
- Management overview and audit

Introduction

It is essential to record the progress of an incident. Incidents may end up in workplace disciplinary action, civil or criminal court or result in investigation by a regulator. Equally, organizations need to learn from incidents – usually via the post-incident review mechanism – and for that to work properly, a decent narrative of the incident must be able to be reconstructed weeks or even months after the critical events.

Equally, an organization of any significant size will have internal and external audit functions that are there to review the effectiveness of aspects of the business. Individual incidents and the overall conduct of the incident management function are likely to have operational, financial and regulatory and legal impacts. Therefore, incident inputs, activities and decisions need to be properly recorded.

Record Keeping

There are a number of different types of records that will need to be kept and how you will need to deal with these is covered in more detail in the next operational part of the book.

At this point, we are concerned with acquiring, constructing or modifying some form of information system for this purpose. Generally, you will need to record:

- Metadata about an incident, including assigning people to the various roles.
- Information and evidence with the ability to add attachments and, ideally the ability to digitally sign them.
- An incident narrative, including reports, possibly as attachments.
- Decisions logs (and, if they are being kept at the per-incident level, risk logs).
- Metrics information.

Records must be quick to make, flexible and have some degree of assurance. The latter will require individual accountability, a reasonable granular level of access control and may require more complex technical assurance measures. To an extent, think of it as a version of a ship's or watch-keeper's log, where you record both standard "daily" information and a list of occurrences.

It is also worth considering a simple notebook. Matthew likes these for a number of reasons, many of them even credible. Ideas occur to people all of the time – on waking from sleep, in the shower, while dozing in a particularly dull project progress meeting. The ability to write the idea down exactly as it was when it occurred to you* can help you and your team decide whether it was actually a "clever idea" or merely a novel one.

Also, within some legal systems, the ability to look back on "contemporaneous notes" can provide a very significant advantage if you are talking to lawyers months or even years after the events occurred.

---

* Even in the shower, if you are that prone to them. The "Rite in the Rain" brand of notebooks and pens will work, but not even Matthew has considered that as appropriate.

However, if you do rely personally or organizationally on some degree of paper note-taking, it is well worth considering transferring these to the main recording system once the opportunity presents itself.

Communications

Nowadays, we take communications for granted. It was not always this way.

The advance of digital and mobile communications systems has been swift and world-changing.

However, for incident response, we need to consider that the communications systems we rely on may themselves be affected by the very information security incident that we are trying to manage.

Provision of out-of-band communications – certainly voice but also potentially data – must be considered as a necessary part of incident management.* The efficient "unified communications" system provided by your IT department may simply be ineffective under directed attack or where the underlying network is swamped or unavailable.

It is also worth noting that major disaster events will also have a significant impact on communications.

Matthew was in Ireland during the 9/11 events, at a conference with many American speakers and attendees. Most people's mobile phones failed – including his. The significant Irish community in New York meant that many thousands of people were phoning to enquire about friends and relatives and being in Ireland, rather than the USA or the UK where most of the attendees were from, meant that the "priority access" phones held by a number of the participants had no special priority on the local mobile networks. Luckily, the security director of one of the Irish banks had a phone with locally recognised priority access. That was handed around quite a lot in the first few hours.

Information Systems

For small organizations, it is entirely possible to manage incidents using a paper or free-text recording system and it is also a pragmatic

---

* This can be considered alongside or as part of the communications provision for the early stages of the organization's disaster recovery process.

approach for very sensitive incidents where the security of any incident recording system is considered insufficient.

However, for organizations that require management information, traceability and auditability, it will be more appropriate to use some form of electronic record. Again, for smaller organizations, a collaboration tool or a secure area within a wider enterprise collaboration environment may be suitable.

Bespoke Incident Management systems are available, either standalone or as part of SIEM suites. Various service management systems also have sufficient flexibility to be used for security incident management, although care needs to be taken in a number of areas. ITIL or ISO20000 systems use somewhat different incident management models to ISO27001 to ensure that sensitive incident data is suitably protected (for example, using DRM on embedded documents) and they are unlikely to offer evidential protection information.

System Requirements

If you are procuring an incident support system, you should consider the following requirements:

- Extensibility
- Strong functional security
- Workflow management
- Integration with SMS* or similar alerting functionality
- Reporting
- Flexible data types

Security The incident management system should be specified so that it can hold and report on very sensitive information – including for internal investigations. This will require a comprehensive set of security functionality requirements:

- Strong link security
- Strong authentication – ideally including two-factor authentication

---

* Practical experience with use of SMS in an incident response scenario indicates that delivery is asynchronous and unreliable. The experience of millions of teenagers, worldwide, indicates that this is not a significant issue.

- Highly granular access control (including tailored views)
- Administrator restrictions
- Strong backup and database journaling
- Evidential controls (for example, time-stamping, digital signatures for attachments, etc.)

Connectivity to the application should be via encrypted and authenticated links and use of strong authentication methods, separately managed from corporate IT systems, should be considered.

Where the investigations team does not have sufficient technical resource to administer its own systems, significant care needs to be taken to ensure that IT support staff cannot gain access to investigations data.* This may require special siting of servers, database record encryption and use of DRM technologies.

Access Control   Generally, it is a reasonably good idea to allow reasonably open access to security incident information – not least because this often stops you from having to take time out of incident management to write and send somebody a report about it. For good reasons, this should only be extended to a relatively trusted community. For a large organization, this might include the security and IT incident handlers (if these are different), appropriate senior IT and operations management and risk and audit staff.

Additional security restrictions (i.e. named individuals only access) to special handling incidents should be considered. Legitimate expectations of privacy, especially where allegations are made against internal or partner organization staff, mean that most data on these incidents should be restricted to the direct investigating team. If a flexible database system is being used, those fields which do not divulge any significant details may be presented to the more general user population. At a minimum, the incident reference, the authorisation for initiation and the contact details for the current incident manager should be available.

---

* In practice, Matthew found that a significant number of allegations were either mistaken or, unfortunately, malicious. Additionally, sensitive personal information about witnesses or victims is regularly uncovered during investigations therefore it is essential that access to investigations data of this sort is restricted to as small a group as possible while maintaining appropriate control and resourcing.

It is also worth, if practical, being able to add a "sensitive information" flag to incident narrative entries (including any relevant attachments) for usually-open incidents which should restrict access both to a tighter user group* and, potentially, to certain groups of computers or methods of connecting to the system front end (for example, from the network rather than via remote VPN). This can be because a particular record, while not indicating any fault, may contain ancillary personal information or customer details that cannot be redacted for evidentiary or other reasons.

Where, for whatever reason, an incident or record is not displayed, it is often appropriate to show a brief metadata summary, for example:

> 13:04 15 Sep 17: 13090135[†] - Special Handling Incident. Incident Manager: M Pemble.

Or, for a sensitive record within a more generally open incident.

> 15:37 20 Sep 15 - Sensitive information record. Created by W Goucher. For access, contact the Incident Manager on ext. 5239.

Alerting   Particularly if your organization will rely on on-call staff rather than having 24×7 shift-working, it is important to have an automated means of alerting the initial responder. Regardless, as a significant part of the incident response team are likely to be on a best endeavours basis for specialist advice and for surge capacity, an alerting mechanism can be very useful.

It should be noted that, as any incident may impact on IP connectivity, that alerting should be configurable to or default to use an out-of-band communications method rather than any integrated VOIP or other IP communications medium. A separate or backup low-bandwidth ISP connection may also be a useful business continuity control.

Reporting   Where an automated system is used, there are multiple levels of reporting that should be easily generated:

- Narrative activity reports for individual incidents.

---

* Usually, just the people directly working on – and sometimes but not always – senior incident managers.
[†] An arbitrary format for the incident number.

- Dashboard or similar over-view reports for incident response activities (for example on a daily, weekly or monthly basis).
- Tracking lists for new, open or recently closed incidents.
- Composite reports for all briefings (for example, management, customer or media) generated during a specific period.
- Composite reports of incident summaries for currently open and recently closed incidents.
- Activity reports for individual team members.*
- Privilege and authorisation audit reports.

The access privileges of the user requesting the reports should also be taken in to account. This can be overt, where only a limited range of reports are available to low privilege users, or covert, where reports only reflect those incidents or data fields to which the user has been granted access. For transparency, a combined restriction is most appropriate but may be difficult to achieve technically.

On-demand or scripted reporting functionality is desirable if large numbers of incidents are expected.

Traceability and Auditability

- All users of the system must have individually allocated accounts.†
- All entries to the incident management system should be time-stamped.
- All entries should be recorded against the incident member ID used. Where anonymous reporting is permitted, such reports should be explicitly tagged as "anonymous."
- All entries must be locked once submitted. Although entry deletion will need to be permitted, this should be subject to strong procedural controls and require use of special privileges to delete the entry. Deleted entries should be replaced with an appropriate justification and link to the user who conducted the deletion.
- Where incident entries may form part of a chain of evidence, the use of digital signatures is recommended.

---

* Necessary, for example, if a critical team member falls ill and their work has to be transferred without a proper handover.
† Multi-user email accounts, for example, for incident alerting are permitted but should be audited to indicate access by specific user accounts.

Broad Data Access

Management Overview and Audit

In larger organizations, the management of incidents is likely to attract a degree of scrutiny from business area and central management and from internal and external auditors. In many cases, although there is a legitimate reason for auditors and other parties to have access to broad data (even metadata) about incidents, there are good privacy and other reasons* for not allowing equivalent access to the details of investigations during their progress and, sometimes, even once an investigation has been concluded.

Designing the system from the outset to be able to produce appropriate dashboards and reports will minimise the time incident managers need to spend away from their core tasks to produce reports.

Dashboards

Your organization will probably already have a collection of IT dashboards and you will generally want to pick something with a familiar look-and-feel for viewing by your business or executive management.

Typically, you might want to include (a week may be a relevant period for you in incident terms – large or unlucky organizations may need to use a day, many organizations we have worked with would get away with using a month.)

Some suggestions for:

- Number of open security incidents
- Number of incidents opened in <period>
- Number of incidents closed in <period>
- Open incident breakdown by priority
- Open incident breakdown by category (if you don't have a very complex categorisation system)

---

* In jurisdictions where there are strong legal or regulatory privacy rights and especially where private information for victims, witnesses or associates of the investigation subjects is recorded, it may be necessary to continue to limit access indefinitely. Or, at least, while that information is retained.

- Number of "executive interest" (or whatever you have decided to call it) incidents
- Number of open incidents not appended or amended in <subset of period> (obviously, because these are incidents that may be considered for closure)

Additionally, if you are large enough to have different business units, it is probably worth being able to filter the reports using this.

If you want to make your incident managers' lives simpler, I would also recommend them being able to tailor a dashboard to themselves.

Reporting

Accordingly, it is appropriate to build in a number of oversight reports to be available. The level of information available on specific incidents should be carefully restricted, especially for special handling incidents, but access to contact details and other metadata and, for standard incidents, to the incident manager's summary should be a reasonable level.

This is suitable for an on-going level of "keeping an eye on ..." Clearly, if you are under management review or subject to a specific audit, you will need to provide more detail. However, this will need to be under careful but independent control. Your Data Protection or Chief Privacy Officer or a senior HR manager may be an appropriate adjudicator.

Audit

As well as the recording for audit functionality noted above, it will also be necessary to configure the system to be able to run various audit reports.

Ad hoc reporting functionality will be needed but a series of pre-configured reports will improve efficiency. Suitable reports will need to include:

- All records for a particular incident number
- All incidents linked to a particular incident number
- All records for a particular incident team member or manager
- All authorisations for a particular incident manager (or team member if they are allowed to authorise)

- All records within a specific date and time range
- All records for a particular business unit

Obviously, allowing combinations of the above by drop-down or similar easy selection process would be an ideal user interface.

Retention Policy

Any recording mechanism will need to allow you to implement a data retention policy.

Some incident data will need to be retained for a significant amount of time – particularly costs, resource requirements, response times and similar metrics that will allow you to do year on year analysis of incident performance. Not least so that you can justify bids for specialist skills or equipment or simply more staff with the relevant training.

In cases where legal or employment disciplinary actions have been taken, retention of all data until a suitable end-point in the legal process has been reached is likely to be required. This will vary depending on your jurisdiction and the precise nature of the actions (and any appeals activity), so consult your Human Resources lawyer or case manager. However, especially as these sorts of cases are very likely to involve personal and sensitive data, you may which to consider archiving the data off-host, with appropriate physical and encryption protection.

In many other cases, you will want to delete much of the incident data after a suitable period. This should fit in with the other information management and retention policies, if your organization has them. Incident data is unlikely to be legally considered as a special case, above other sensitive material held by most organizations, such as employee health records and appraisal reports.

Revealing the Case Studies

Amber Inc.

Is at the point in its development where it has the opportunity to keep good records from the earliest point of their IR capability. As the function develops, there will be approaches that work well, some that fail and some that seem to be ok at the moment but change needs to be planned. In this modern age of employment mobility, they cannot rely on the members of the IR group remaining the same or having perfect recall of situations and the background behind decisions being taken. It is for all these reasons that keeping records is so important because the reasons why an action is taken is as important as why it isn't.

Also, in their movement towards accreditation to ISO27001:2013 they will need to have any established process for recording incidents and their handling. Some organizations only begin to make that a formal process when they are preparing for accreditation but putting the process in place from the early days of IR means that, by the time they apply for accreditation the records they have, and the uses these are put to is an established and mature, and mostly likely to be well understood by all key personnel who may be contacted during the accreditation process. In other words, it's one less thing to worry about.

Jade Ltd.

Is in a slightly different position from Amber Inc. in that it doesn't have the motivation of approaching accreditation to spur them into action. However, they are likely to find themselves being audited by or on behalf of their customers. In recent years, there has been a growing realisation that passing off responsibly for security of data by delegating that care to a third party; often, as in this case, a data centre. Back in 2008, The Royal Bank of Scotland found itself at the centre of an investigation into the selling of old computers on eBay* without their hard discs being removed and securely destroyed. They were not alone, other organizations such as Amex found they were vulnerable to the same problem. It had come about when their contractors had failed to prevent one of their staff taking a computer and selling it on eBay themselves. Although the bank was not at fault it was their name, not that of the contractor, that grabbed the headlines. This was the time when public trust in the banking sector in the UK was low and so a story such as this just fed a hunger for more stories that reenforced that lack of trust. What RBS and other organizations that process sensitive information have had to do is to audit the security of their contractors

---

* http://www.dailymail.co.uk/news/article-1049121/Government-probe-launched-details-million-bank-customers-sold-eBay.html. Viewed on 1st December 2015.

on a regular basis. If Jade Ltd. has not already been subject to such a check, it will do before much longer. This especially because of the sensitivity of some of the information they hold.

When these audits take place, they must expect that the auditor will be looking for proof not only of the existence of suitable controls, but also of how these controls are carried out and how incidents are logged and dealt with. Organizations with significant public profiles cannot afford to be associated with contractors whose operations are not up to their own standard with regard to the handling sensitive data. Those who fail are likely to find themselves loosing good customers.

Jade Ltd. needs to ensure that they focus on secure processing and ensure they understand the need for security that their customers are increasingly calling for. If they do that, then they may even find themselves being a data centre that people switch to, rather than from. Secure processes and controls are an important selling point for the foreseeable future so time and money spent getting these right now will undoubtedly bring good returns in the future.

13

MANAGING THE BACKSTAGE CREW

And he sailed back over a year
and in and out of weeks
and through a day
and into the night of his very own room
where he found his supper waiting for him
and it was still hot.

Maurice Sendak
Where the Wild Things Are

Information in this chapter:

- Why and how of caring for IR team
- Who are the backstage crew
- What is the role of the backstage crew – valuing the backstage crew
- Communication and expectations
- The strains of extended IR work on life
- Reward and recognition.
- Lessons in Amber Inc. context
- Lessons in Jade Ltd. context
- Summary

Introduction

The main focus of this book is rightly focused on preparing for and dealing with incidents, but to look at that exclusively is to miss a key element. Incident response, especially out of hours, is a process that affects not only the team members, but also those they live with or

117

regularly socialise with. The disruption can go from minor irritation to social embarrassment. In some cases, even to causing conflict as different aspects of the team member's life compete for attention and priority. As the development and nurturing of an effective incident response team can be challenging pressures that can lead to staff resigning from IR work are best understood and, where possible, addressed.

What's the Fuss About?

When my dad was a young construction manager, the main site he was responsible for was a favourite with any local youth who wanted to make fire or any other kind of mischief at night, especially at weekends. Our house phone rang at all hours and Dad would be in his car and off to deal with problems before I really realised what was happening. I do remember Mum having to make adjustments to plans and sometimes meals because of the calls. I used to get annoyed at the loud phone waking me, and Dad being grumpy with lack of sleep. However, I was taught very firmly that this disruption was a key part of his job and he put the food on the table so the rest of us had to adapt. Those were the 1960s, when a "breadwinner and housewife" family structure was much more common with activities often organised around the needs of the breadwinner.

Today things are much more complex in many households, often with more than one earner in a household and also an increasing number having care responsibilities for both young and elderly relatives. This may include hands-on care as well as balancing external care providers and the job requirements of more than one adult household member. However, it should also be considered that many live alone and have nobody to put food in front of them at the end of a long day, which can be good or bad depending on the day.

In planning an incident management team, consider the following repercussions for the family and friend structure surrounding the team.

- Long hours
- Effect of fatigue on relationships
- The need for availability to team
- The lack of availability to family and friends

- The movement of focus and priority from home to work
- Disruption to established schedules in personal life
- Neglect of personal life
- Difficulty of winding down from incidents

All of these are important and some of them are potentially very serious but are, to an experienced manager, predictable to a certain extent. Let me offer you some additional problems which may not be so obvious.

Money

In the first instance, there is the matter of extra overtime payments for incident response, especially out of hours, work. This is entirely necessary and appropriate, and indeed can be a big help in balancing household budgets. However, it can lead to a situation whereby staff become trapped in the team by the need to keep earning at the higher level, even when other pressures make it difficult to continue the work.

Ubiquitous Communication

In the early days of working in incident management, Matthew almost always had a pager device on his belt. An incident was often signalled by a message and which meant he then had to either go somewhere that had a good mobile phone signal* or find a landline phone. As a result, long car journeys and even shopping trips to places where signal strength was unknown resisted. Realistically, it was possible to make short trips as long as we accepted I might, for example, be doing circuits of the supermarket while Matthew was stood outside in the rain trying to get the incident stabilised until he could get home. This was before smartphones and reliable WiFi and you might think that makes it better. Maybe.

Anyone involved in managing an incident response team will tell you that you are only really off duty when you are in the air.† Otherwise, mobile phones and computing means you are always

---

* Hard to believe that until relatively recently our house had significant black spots for signal coverage, and we live less than 30 miles from a major UK city.
† And that is now changing with more modern planes with some airlines.

within reach. Picture the scene. We are on a family holiday, which was not common for us. We were in the hills of Crete and it was calm, peaceful and restful away from resorts and daily bustle, which is what we all very much needed. Our eldest had got a little sunburnt the day before, so wanted to watch a DVD in the cool of indoors. When the TV was switched on, the default screen was a news channel and that was showing a scene of devastation centred on what was left of a red London bus. The date was 7th July 2005 and this must have been amongst the first pictures broadcast, as it was early in the day. Because some of the bank offices were in London, I called Matthew to the screen and he immediately turned on his mobile phone and started trying to contact people. We might have thought we were out of touch – not at all, as it turned out. He was able contact his staff, reassure himself that all were safe and make contingency arrangements for accommodation overnight in case transport was still static at the end of the day. The urgency was increased by the knowledge that communication was likely to get harder if the situation escalated and the mobile network availability was prioritised to the emergency services. Had he found out about the incident but been unable to make contact, he would have been worried and distracted and that would have reduced the effectiveness of the holiday as a way of unwinding. Yes, we lost a morning while he was on the phone, however, as all staff were safe, he was able to begin relaxing again by the afternoon. But on the other hand, that was our holiday and we were in need to some time away from incident response. In this case, it was a mixed blessing, but it was an example of mobile communication as a double-edged tool.

Now not only is the mobile phone signal more reliable, but WiFi and cellular signals to laptop, tablet and smartphone means that the IR team member can carry their desk with them almost everywhere. No more confinement waiting for an incident call, but then again work is never far away, even when they are not on call.

Social

In this digital age, we can easily consider that all incidents can be handled from a combination of phone and computer access. In some situations, however, that is not the case. Sometimes these matters cannot be dealt with remotely, they need action on the ground, and that can lead to problems for those caught in the wake. We were once at a weekend conference in Perth, Scotland. Matthew wasn't on call. Well, technically not, anyway. As we looked across the conference centre's garden, lightly touched by the first of the early morning autumnal colours, the pager buzzed. It was the bank and there was a problem, a significant one. By the time breakfast was served, Matthew was off on his 42-mile journey to the main office in Edinburgh and I was left to make his apologies and hope that he could get back in time for us to leave on the Sunday morning.

As it turned out, he arrived back on Saturday evening, tired and hungry, having had no breakfast and little lunch. An early morning "wake up and smile" intervention on Sunday that saw people banging on our bedroom door with tambourines and over caffeinated smiles nearly ended in a bloodbath. Though well meaning, the culprits just couldn't understand why this wasn't received with fun and laughter. It was 7:30 a.m. – go figure! The rest of the conference was lost on Matthew, both in the sense that he needed to keep in touch with the incident, and the spent time away meant he was alienated from the culture and atmosphere of the event. I had tried to explain what was happening to our friends, although my ability to satisfy the understandable curiosity was limited, as with any security incident at a major bank, because details couldn't be shared. For all my efforts, I don't think that most of our fellow delegates really appreciated why we had allowed the incident to affect our experience of the weekend. In short, the incident ruined the event for us.

*There Were Three of Us in This Marriage, So It Was a Bit Crowded**

This is probably the most famous royal quote of recent years[†] and might sound a bit over dramatic in the context of incident response. But when your close friend, or spouse or partner or significant other is on the phone for hours at a time and becomes totally absorbed in the ongoing incident, it can feel like that. There is a psychological concept called

---

[*] BBC Panorama Interview with Diana, Princess of Wales by Martin Bashir, November 1995

[†] Which rather depends on whether you are old enough for 1995 to be "recent years" to you, I suppose.

"cognitive absorption," which is when the user becomes so absorbed in something they don't notice what is going on around them. Watch people play *Angry Birds* and you will get a flavour. In layman's terms, people have a "limited bandwidth" of concentration brainpower to work with. If we are focused on something, maybe a phone call in a noisy environment the brain narrows focus on the core function and sort of fades signals from other non-critical sources (you would probably notice a fire alarm). This can lead to those involved in very absorbing incidents overlook or forget matters that are on the outside of the immediate event. Such things could be as trivial as forgetting to pick up some milk on the way home or as important as forgetting you have guests coming for dinner.* These sort of things can chip away at any relationship, whether caused by IR work or not, but where the root cause is able to be assigned to IR then that can be seen as the element that is keeping the person from their relationship.

Our record to date was the 36-hour conference call that was mentioned earlier. The length of the call was necessitated by a requirement by senior management for regular updates in the form of hourly meetings. While this was reasonable under the circumstances, the problem arose because the meetings took between 50 and 55 minutes, sometimes longer; hence, they ran into each other leading to a continuous forum. Short naps were grabbed, often more by body than mind, and meals were eaten one-handed, mobile phone clamped to the other ear, and I had the vital job of left keeping an ear open and taking notes during comfort breaks. Neither of us got much sleep. Matthew couldn't take more than the briefest shower and shave, and there was little conversation between us or with the children. Also, I couldn't take the car anywhere in case Matthew had to go into the office at short notice. In short, the whole family were entangled in the whirlpool of the incident and we could only ride along. By the end, humour and temper was very short and the working week had only just started.

The incident concluded after the start of the week, which compounded the problem for me because I had become involved in the incident but had no closure. Once Matthew came home in the evening, he certainly didn't want to talk about it. Understandably,

---

* Neither of which, I hasten to add, Matthew has been guilty of thus far.

he just wanted to eat and sleep and chat about other things. It was frustrating, almost like someone was holding back the last chapter of an engrossing book.

Irrational as it seems, out-of-hours IR work can lead to a feeling of competition for attention between work and home. Of course, it has to be admitted that family and friends, with all their day to day dramas and drudgery, could struggle to compete with the problem solving and other potentially exciting challenges of incident response. Incidents have understandable causes and solvable, or at least the effects can be mitigated. Social or family dramas, despite what soap operas might portray, tend not to be solvable in a few minutes or hours, if ever. How can real life compete? Where the competition between incident response and life is not handled in a balanced way, there is an increased likelihood of pressure to give up the glamorous competition that is the IR team. This sort of pressure is on you, as an incident response team manager, you want to avoid if at all possible.

Working with the Unspeakable

Security incident response is often about fraud, IT-based attacks and HR issues such as bullying. However, there is another side that can be very unpleasant. This is more likely where the organization is large, both because there are more users on the system and also because users are more likely to believe their activities will be lost in the everyday noise of business. I'm talking about pornography and indecency. It is, thankfully, hard for those of us who have not seen the worst kind of material to really appreciate how bad it can be. I heard of a situation once where a HR manager fainted when he insisted on viewing some such images. There is an extent to which those who have to view this type of material become desensitised, but then again, I suspect fewer actually do than assert they have. Why can this be a problem?

Let's consider a fictional example. A man is working on an incident management team at a large multinational company. A number of the staff are found to be exchanging images of violent pornography involving teenage girls, and this team member is assigned to the incident. In the course of the incident, very unpleasant images have to be viewed and categorised. At the end of a tough day, one that he doesn't want to think about, let alone talk about with his family, he is just unwinding in front of the television. His 13-year-old daughter comes into the room to show her parents the new outfit she bought for the local youth club Christmas party. It is shorter than they might like, but is not, by standard of her peers, overly revealing. However, our team member sees how much she resembles some of the images he has been looking at, including the pattern of her clothing. It makes him angry and he explodes in a fit of temper, saying that she is banned from going out in that outfit, and the storm gates that had held back all the disgust and upset are breached and there is no holding back. The daughter and her mum are distraught at this inexplicable and uncharacteristic reaction. The team member feels confused and upset. It would not take too many events like this before the team could to lose a key member.

The standard modern answer is to say that the team members need to talk about how they are feeling, but who should they talk to? Their family and friends? Why would they want to spread the knowledge they have? Why spread the pain when all they want is to forget the images? It is easy to see how alcohol might be used by some as a way of reducing the vibrancy of the images, but that can, in some cases, lead to still greater problems without actually solving the original one. Later, we will discuss about how incident management can set matters in hand that will help the team cope with traumatic situations like this, but this chapter is considering the "backstage crew" – those who get caught in the eye of this sort of storm. It has to be recognised that, for some, the impact is significant and they should not feel isolated from help themselves or they become potential victims of the event, too.

The Role of the Backstage Crew

If you have ever watched or worked with a backstage crew at a music, dance or drama performance, you will know that they are critical to the ability of the performers to do their thing. Whether it is moving scenery, getting lighting and sound up and running, preparing and maintaining costumes or making sure that everyone has enough of the sort of food and drink they need or should have, all require planning and effort and contingency management by every crew member. Any crew who work around the performance area will tend to wear black or other colour that blends in and helps them to appear invisible. The backstage crew for members of your incident response teams are similarly vital and ideally invisible. They certainly should not be getting in the way of the work if possible, but their organising of food and moving the metaphorical furniture when the team member is operating from outside of work is vital. Sometimes, however, it can be hard to know what the required response is as a crewmember. Many years ago, I was a young wife visiting the Royal Naval College, Dartmouth, England for a special "Wives Weekend." Over the two days, we were strongly briefed about the fact that the ability of the officers to do their job was greatly dependent on the wives providing strong support at home.* The problem was that through all the presentations and talks and other events of the weekend, nobody would tell us exactly what "support" entailed, only that our husbands' effectiveness and career progression depended on us doing it correctly. Instead of being reassuring, it was depressing, as we were left feeling like we were at sea without charts or a rudder.

So What Can They Do?

Maintenance   Most incidents will take place in the working week and will be coped with in the normal way with, hopefully, give and take with those in the incident response team being supported by those in the wider incident management team. However, if there is a significant incident, especially when it leads to out-of-hours working, the need for good maintenance is real. When someone is concentrating on a task, there is less chance they will have time to prepare, or even eat, complicated meals. They need nourishing food that will keep up their energy levels and help them to think clearly. Likewise, the importance of hydration has been studied a great deal in recent years, particularly with regard to the academic performance of children in school. So, it is clear that IR team members will need effective fluids, although, fairly obviously, alcohol should be kept to moderate levels to keep reasoning clear. In some cases, there may be policy guidelines regarding alcohol consumed by someone working out-of-hours on an incident. This is largely because of the effect on judgment and the fact it might make

---

* If this sounds sexist and archaic, I should say this was the mid-80s – and yes, it was.

the team member unable to legally drive to manage an incident from another location.

Social One of the frustrating things about being on call for IR is being restricted as to being able to mix with friends. In many instances, nothing will actually happen during the duty period and they have missed out on social stuff for no good reason. So, try to fit some events around their being able to slip out or stay sober enough to deal with work, if necessary. The ease of mobile communication makes this easier, but it would be best if the worst-case scenario of the team member having to withdraw from the event part way through was considered and allowed for.

Teflon Coated IR can be frustrating – really, really frustrating. Chasing phone calls, being put on hold and being passed from pillar to post trying to deal with a phishing attack or getting advice about software from vendors out of hours can all build the pressure. The trick with being a good member of the crew is to realise that you may well be caught in the fallout. The team member may become annoyed with their crew just because they are there, rather than because they have done anything wrong. It would be true to say team members shouldn't get annoyed with their crew, but they will, and crew will get annoyed back. However, just like the theatre best stage crew, the IR crew have to learn to let it run off them without taking it too personally.

Taking a Break This is important for everyone, but for those who loose weekends to out-of-hours IR work, it is especially important. IR work can be very absorbing and, for some, addictive. The problem is that real world perspective, and properly rested team members, are vital, and they need to take proper breaks to get that. It need not be extravagant; a weekend visiting friends or having them to stay may be enough. I would suggest this is particularly important where someone lives alone and doesn't have a lot of outside interests, but it is a very individual thing.

Sharing the Experience For the backstage crew, the problems that arise can be compounded by the impression that they are the only ones experiencing the issues that arise. I found that the real benefit of living in naval accommodation was that those around me understood problems that might arise and listening and active support was something that many contributed to and benefited from. Once off base, it was very different. Crews can often find that an appropriate social event can be helpful in this. It can help at the very basic level to be able to put human faces on the names of people who they may speak to on the phone quite often. It can sometimes be an opportunity for the boss of the incident response team to be available to listen to complaints or comments. I knew a manager once who believed he benefited from meeting the families in relaxed BBQ-type events, as it gave him the chance to understand a little more of the situation his team member was in and the sort of support they were getting. It wasn't a situation to judge the crew, it was a way of understanding better. Although social events can cost significantly, this can be offset against recruiting and training new team members in some cases.

Payback   One large organization I heard of gave staff who had significant responsibilities for out-of-hours work "family experience" vouchers. It was felt that these were more likely to be used as a reward for the whole crew, rather than just relying on extra payment which may be absorbed in the household budget. The crew I encountered were very pleased by it and felt it was a real sign of respect for the inconvenience and stress that the work occasionally caused the family.

Managing the Performance   The message I would want to send from this chapter is that successful incident management can be difficult for a wider group than those seen in the workplace. Particularly where the organization is large or the incident rate is high, particularly in incidents that impact on out of hours working, a manager needs to understand the range of pressures and how they can be managed in order to provide the operational support the organization requires.

Revealing the Case Studies

Amber Inc.

This organization has probably had this function operating for a while, but not in the sense of formal IM. As such, their information maturity about the likely impact on the crew of IA should be much higher. It should be possible to predict the level of demand on the IM team, at least in its early days. This will help to judge likely crew impact and the extent to which their role needs to be considered in the early days.

Jade Ltd.

In this organization, incident response is something they are being forced into to a certain extent by the requirements of customers. They only have a very small IT department, which is likely to provide the majority of the internal IM team. How much the team will operate, the nature of the incidents and how much that will impact on their crew will be difficult to assess at the outset. It is likely that the most useful approach by the IM head is to keep the issues in mind as the development of the team is assessed. If there comes a point where there is significant external impact from incidents, then some of the issues raised here may need to be addressed.

14

DEALING WITH
EXTERNAL AGENCIES

I think the problem, to be quite honest with you, is that you've never really known what the question is.

Douglas Adams
Life, the Universe and Everything

Information in this chapter:

- Law enforcement
- Internet service providers
- Making and maintaining contact
- A little about the law
- Incident co-operation organizations

Introduction

Many incidents have sources or impacts outside your organization and for numerous incident types, you will not have the appropriate access or may be legally prohibited from conducting a sufficient investigation. Also, it is common, particularly when you are setting up your organization but extending even to the most mature and experienced incident teams, to need to acquire expert advice and assistance from external parties.

Accordingly, it is well worth building up relationships with appropriate external agencies before you need them in a rush.

Who, What and Why

Law Enforcement

Your relationship with law enforcement will need to take careful account of your organizational culture. Some organizations are very happy to have an open, two-way communication with law enforcement, and to co-operate in the reporting and prosecution of suspected crimes. Other organizations, whether for sartorial reasons or because of jurisdictional limitations, will only co-operate with law enforcement following formal legal request or serving of an appropriate warrant. Regardless, as an incident response manager, it is worth getting to know your local cybercrime or computer crime team and in order to more fully understand their capabilities and priorities.

Even if you are keen to report cybercrime, often it will be below the level of social priority at which scarce police forensic and investigations capacity would usually be released. Obviously, if you are unfortunate enough to get caught up in any of the current "horsemen of the internet apocalypse," for example terrorism, child abuse and drugs, possibly also money laundering, (fake news might also count as one – "pestilence," maybe?; however, it is less likely to attract police attention), you may get far more attention than you would be happy with. Having an established relationship of mutual understanding and trust in each other's expertise may find it easier to get much more immediate and enthusiastic response at a point ahead of formal recognition of the seriousness of an event. A well-established prior relationship can even help curb of that enthusiasm such that you can preserve service availability, rather than having critical servers seized to moulder at the back of an evidence locker. Sometimes this can be a two-way street, loaning a newly-trained forensic technician to assist in law enforcement work will give them a much broader experience than merely becoming very familiar with your standard laptop and desktop builds.

Internet Service Providers (ISPs)

When any aspect of your investigation is outside your directly-controlled network, you are likely to need help. One of the more useful sources of information and assistance should be your ISP. They may be able to give you routing information for specific attack sources, work with their peers to throttle (or "black hole") DDoS and similar nuisance attacks and put you in touch with partner organizations that can help you conduct remote investigations. They may also be willing to act as a "trusted introducer" and more extreme circumstances, as translator, for foreign law enforcement and ISPs.

It is well worth understanding the extent of their monitoring and protective controls that could be implemented within a reasonable period, even if you don't currently purchase those services.

ISPs, however, will be operating under certain equipment limitations. They usually run a light monitoring and recording system. Although there are a number of government initiatives aimed at requiring them to retain more data, as you ramp up the level of monitoring or auditing required from a network device, you can significantly impact its ability to do its main role of pushing packets out of one of its connections. Larger devices have separate processing capacity, or even separate modules to ensure that audit requirements do not adversely affect normal performance.

In all, barring the largest or most specialist organizations, it is likely that you are a commodity purchaser of ISP services, therefore the level of flexibility they have (or are willing to indulge on your behalf) may be quite limited. And you need to ensure that the appropriate level of willingness to engage is prepared beforehand, through the appropriate supplier and account management contacts.

Also check on the ISP that provides your domain name services. Your main ISP will probably, but not always, provide resolving DNS. However, your authoritative DNS may be provided elsewhere or ideally, by a mixed set of providers. Again, identify appropriate contacts and develop an understanding of their capability and limitations. Also, their ability (and willingness) to provide you with information or to make changes to mitigate the impact of an attack should be explored prior to needing help.

Regulators

As with law enforcement, it is often useful to have a relationship with your regulatory authorities, whoever they are, before you need to make a report to them. The wider business may well already have contact points, and you should work through these initially even if you are not in a formally regulated sector. You should be aware that certain aspects of your business, for example data protection, may still be subject to formal regulation.

The EU GDPR requires relevant incidents to be reported within 72 hours. Understanding exactly who your regulator is, what they expect in the initial and subsequent reports, and the best methods of communicating with them should be done long before you have to make that hurried and intensely political step of divulging an organizational failure to a regulator with extensive abilities to fine, and otherwise sanction, your organization. This may indeed be openly available on their website but it is always worth establishing some degree of personal rapport.

Other regulators will have different focuses and requirements. Understanding these before the event, and potentially being able to prepare templates will allow you to focus investigations in such a way that ensures the right information is captured to allow you to answer anticipated regulatory concerns. It should also help limit additional requests for more detailed analysis and reporting.

A Little Bit about the Law

The odd and often painful conjunction between information security (a complex and important area, populated by often strangely dressed people insisting on using a weird jargon full of unnecessary neologisms and excruciating acronyms) and the law (a complex and important area populated by often strangely dressed people insisting on using a weird jargon full of words from long-dead languages and references to the distant past) is vital as far as investigations management and practice is concerned.

However, we are not lawyers, even barrack-room ones, and therefore this book, as with any good computer system, will be obsolescent if not obsolete by the time it arrives at your desk should never be considered as legal advice. A source of lots of good hints, hopefully, but no substitute for proper legal advice.

In fact, as we have no idea where you are reading this, it is quite possible that we don't even know a lawyer who is qualified to practice in your jurisdiction.

If You Are in an Incident and Have a Legal Problem –
Go and Find Yourself a Good Lawyer

If you are in an incident and don't have a legal problem, have another check around if you've got time – they do hide in somewhat unexpected places – and find yourself a good lawyer.

If you are not in an incident, great, but take the time that gives you to make sure that you find yourself a good lawyer.

In fact, unless your company is particularly parochial for this modern era, you are going to need access to lawyers in a variety of jurisdictions. If your corporate lawyers are part of or allied to one of the global law firms, this is relatively easy (if rather expensive). Otherwise, take advice.

What Is a Good Lawyer?

To quote an American law blogger:

> A good lawyer's loyalty lies in being ready to give plain-spoken advice that will get you fired if your client's in the wrong mood. An effective advocate's loyalty isn't about saying 'Good idea' or 'You're right,' it's about warning 'Shut up' and 'No, you shouldn't do that' and 'Yes, I understand you want to do that, but here's why it's a terrible idea.' Real loyalty looks like Cordelia, refusing to flatter King Lear at great cost, not like her sisters, praising him effusively to get more land.
>
> **Ken White (@Popehat)**

But that's probably not much help to you. More specifically, you are going to need somebody (or somebodies) with a range of the following:

- Knowledge of your regulatory sector (if you, or your customers, are operating within one or more).
- Contracts law (particularly for IT services).
- Criminal law (particularly around hacking, fraud and harassment).
- Employment law.
- Data protection law.
- Intellectual property rights law.
- Access to advice on foreign law and law enforcement powers and obligations.

- Access to some form of out-of-hours or on-call assistance, albeit probably at a lower level of specialist competence.

And, especially difficult to find

- Knowledge of the extent and limitations of a company's rights to conduct investigations.

Please note that legal jurisdictions involve some obscure boundaries, as well as the more obvious ones. Data protection law, for example, was, prior to GDPR, significantly common amongst the EEA nations, but with some notable differences.* US law is considered to apply extra-territorially more than many other nations insist and varies not only across state and county lines but also with US Federal Court of Appeals districts, and the UK runs three entirely separate legal systems – England and Wales,† Northern Ireland and Scotland – the latter running on a completely different construction of law, hailing back to a Roman, rather than feudal model.

Incident Co-Operation Organizations

Very often, incidents will involve systems outside of your power to control or to even to gain necessary information from. Although you might involve law enforcement, even if your incident meets their standards for investigation, their legal powers are often quite limited‡ outside their jurisdiction.

Luckily, this is a problem for incident response teams throughout the world and there are a number of co-operative groups that will assist you or can enable introductions to people who can assist you in a wide variety of areas.

The grandpapa of these is the Federation of Incident Response and Security Teams, usually known by its acronym, FIRST. Their members included government and national computer and emergency

---

* The UK's case law in Durant versus FSA and the Italian insistence that a company counts as a person and its data deserves equal protection, as examples.
† Of course, with the Welsh Assembly now having limited law-making powers, English and Welsh law will begin to diverge. Possibly in some materially important areas.
‡ Even with the passing of the US CLOUD Act and the presumed bilateral law enforcement access treaties that are intended to follow based on that act.

response teams, major ISPs, international banks and a variety of other organizations of all shapes and sizes.

We cannot recommend this organization highly enough. Whilst the contact details of member teams are openly available* to the public, the networking and training opportunities available to members are well worth considering. Although the requirements for full team membership may be a little much if you are just beginning to establish your team, there is also the option of individual "Liaison" membership.

There are other services available in different areas of the world. Within Europe, the Géant Trusted Introducer[†] project (which used to run under the Terena banner) provides services to member teams only, but also makes a list of accredited and candidate teams available.[‡] The UK-only CiSP[§] scheme, run by the National Cyber Security Centre also provides the ability to share information about an attack and seek advice and help.

Although we are not aware of any equivalent North American scheme, with the USA, the FBI's InfraGard programme could provide a useful avenue for both obtaining and having an authority verify you to contacts.

However, do not forget the potential for using more general security industry bodies such as ISC[2] or ISACA. Although they do not particularly specialise in incident assistance, both have public forums where you can seek help or contacts in specific organizations or industry areas.

Revealing the Case Studies

Amber Inc. and Jade Ltd.

This is one instance when there is very little difference between the positions of the two companies. Neither could be described as "big Players" by reason of size, particular risk (such as the nuclear industry) or specific local concern, which might make them the particular

---

* https://www.first.org/members/teams/

[†] https://www.trusted-introducer.org

[‡] https://www.trusted-introducer.org/directory/alpha_LICSA.html

[§] Cyber Security Information Sharing Partnership – No, I don't know how they got to the acronym "CiSP" from those words, but CSISP was probably too confusing with CISSP. https://www.ncsc.gov.uk/cisp

concern of their ISP or local law enforcement. Law enforcement might be happy to discuss matters, but this is unlikely to affect their actions in favour of the organization as the interests of Amber Inc. and Jade Ltd. are simply not going to be a priority.

The question is then, how can such organizations acquire the influence and understanding that might be useful in this situation? The easiest approaches may well be through networking and, most especially through recruitment. A classic example is the recruitment of ex-police officers in a range of security, physical or cyber, depending on their skills. Not only would they have some knowledge of the attitude and approach of law enforcement in different situations, they may also probably still have contacts within their ex-organization, which they can use where appropriate.

In terms of networking, this may be through membership of formal industry and special interest groups or attendance at business networking events. Either of these can be helpful, but it is important to be clear what sort of contact is being sought and why, or else while many business cards are collected, this does not reflect the success in terms of getting access to the people desired. IT may still be necessary to follow up with the contact to establish whether they can provide the information and relationship desired.

One cautionary note is to overlook the influence and knowledge that a sales person might profess to have. It is worth remembering that, quite rightly, their motivation is to sell a product or service. Some may, in trying to get the outcome they want, portray their influence and knowledge as being better than it would manifest in practice.

Careful hunting for the right contact, like hunting anything, requires knowledge, patience and a willingness to leave potential pray that are not what is required.

15

TRAINING, QUALIFICATION AND CERTIFICATION

Excellence is an art won by training and habituation. We do not act rightly because we have virtue or excellence, but we rather have those because we have acted rightly. We are what we repeatedly do. Excellence, then, is not an act but a habit.

Aristotle

Information in this chapter:

- Training teams and individuals
- Carnegie Mellon
- FIRST
- SANS
- CESG
- PCIDSS
- Vendors

Introduction

With something as potentially critical to an organization as incident response, it may seem to be common sense that team members are appropriately trained and certified. However, as currently there is no legal or regulatory requirement of staff conducting IR work, then the requirement is often overlooked. This can be a particular problem where the IR function has evolved from an established information security function, especially where the organization is small so most of the IR staff would probably remain primarily in the IT functional area. In such a situation, it can be difficult to identify the point where formal steps need to be taken to ensure staff acquire and develop their IR knowledge and skills. The point at which these steps move from peer to peer training to more formal training, delivered by a subject matter expert, can be difficult to identify; let alone justify in terms of budget of time and money. However, delaying until a deficiency becomes clear in an incident situation may prove to be a false economy. If an incident results in a court case, the legitimacy and credibility given to evidence delivered by an IR team member who lacks formal qualifications can be significantly reduced. In a worst-case situation, it can be so undermined as to be of no use at all. Indeed, the lack of preemptive training can give a negative impression of the overall competence of the team.

This chapter will discuss a number of training areas and certifications, their purpose and the likely value that someone going through that training could be expected to add to their team. While different organizations may look at different training, the important message of this chapter is that formal training in one or more IR skills is essential for anyone who is likely to lead the response to an incident, and very desirable for the rest of the team.

Individual Training

When considering specialist training, a number of important questions need to be considered. These include whether there is sufficient requirement for people with that skill to require a member of staff either to add it to their skill set or become specialist in a particular area. A good example of this is digital forensics. Some medium-to-large organizations still find that the requirement to be able to investigate using these tools is infrequent and therefore doesn't justify a part time or dedicated member of staff. In this case, the skill can be drawn in on an ad hoc basis.

It is important to realise that bringing in an external consultant to help with an incident doesn't necessarily mean that there is no requirement to have an understanding of the knowledge area internally. Connecting members of the team with some specialist training, possibly in different areas, may be more useful. If the organization intends to use consultants for deep specialist tasks, such as digital forensics, having the knowledge in the team regarding how data must be collected in order that any evidence collected could, if necessary, be used in a subsequent criminal case, is essential, i.e. have someone with "first responder" knowledge, where a specialist consultant is used can prevent simple but significant errors being made early on. As part of developing a good relationship with such contractors, holding a discussion with them with regard to the sort of training they feel would be mutually beneficial could pay a high dividend.

Incident response is very much a team deliverable, but this partly comprises from having members of the team with appropriate knowledge in relevant specialist areas such as network analytics and insider threats. Depending on the individual situation, then this may be achieved by training a member of staff to become that specialist or by recruiting a trained and experienced new staff member. If a team is either full-time or housed in a department such as Information Technology where such skills would be in regular use, then it may be cost effective to recruit, rather than just train such skills into the team. In doing that, the employer only needs to ensure that the specialist has access to the sort of training or other knowledge-base events (such as specialist conferences) that will keep their knowledge up to date. However, if the team is small or drawn from a number of teams and therefore would only be used occasionally, then providing training for an current member of staff generally makes more sense.

It is important to appreciate that some organizations can be concerned that their potentially expensive training investment for staff increases the likelihood that training staff would find it easier to take those skills to a new position in a different organization. After all, one of the suggestions above is that a trained and experienced contractor being recruited. As a result, some organizations have a payback clause, which generally means that should a member of staff receive significant training they are expected to use that skill in to the benefit of their employer for a fixed period of time. If they leave before that time is complete, then they may be liable to repay some or all of the cost of that training. However, the manager has a role to play in avoiding staff looking for another job. Where they endeavour to provide a work environment that both values staff members and allows them to develop their skills and abilities, there is less incentive for colleagues to look to move to another employer. Likewise, a situation where staff are regularly expected to carry out tasks that they are inadequately trained for, with no prospect of that gap being addressed, is one where retention becomes a concern. It is important to recognise that there will always be those who will leave their job for a variety of reasons, some of which relate more to their personal life than their professional, and these reasons should be considered outside normal retention concerns, especially in relation to training.

Below, a range of courses and approaches are highlighted. This is neither an exclusive list, nor a list based on rigorous evaluation of course options available. They are courses that our experience has proved to be of a reliable standard. They will also indicate some ideas of the options available at this time. It is advisable that advice with regard to the applicability of these courses in your situation is sought. This may be a good use of business networks and links.

Carnegie Mellon University

Carnegie Mellon has a specialist Software Engineering Institute eLearning portal which can be used to access specialist courses on subjects such as digital forensics and assessing security risk. It is worth remembering, however, that these courses come out of the USA, and so it may be necessary to identify how the member of staff can infill knowledge of relevant UK and EU guidelines and legislation.

SANS Institute

These courses are certainly very technical. There is a lot of detailed delivery covering all areas of incident response and management. There are courses across the UK and US, and there is also online material. The classroom-style courses generally constitute four to six days of very intensive study. With the higher-level courses, there is an exam at the end to check the learning. With such intensive courses, a participant would benefit from the preparation of establishing what knowledge that they would be assumed to have in order to make the course cost effective. Contacting the institute in advance of booking will also help to ensure the best fit between candidate and course.

Certifications

GCHQ / NCSC

GCHQ (and its cyber defence component, NCSC) is a critical government organization in terms of protection against information security and latterly cyberattack. Given their importance to government, they hold a unique position in providing guidance and instruction for the full range of organizations within the UK. In terms of quality control of security courses, they work with the CREST scheme to ensure quality of delivery from authorised training courses that are designed to be appropriate for standard organizations in the public and private sector. They also provide the NCSC/CPNI Cyber Incident Response Scheme for those organizations that have a critical role in the national infrastructure.

It is important that an organization contemplating a NCSC certification understands its risks and the costs of those risks, so as to ensure the cost against benefit is appropriate to the organization. The courses are provided by a number of different training organizations so, again, a preemptive discussion with a provider in order to get the best match between your organizations' need and their delivery. Where the organization doesn't have a good existing experience with any of the providers, then it is worthwhile looking for recommendations, in extremist from customers the course deliverer can provide contact with.

PCIDSS: The Payment Card Industry Data Security Standard

This standard is required in the UK by any organization that handles card payments. Many small businesses use a third party, such as PayPal or a bank to process sensitive customer data and therefore don't have to meet the more exacting standards they may otherwise be subject to. However, it is still important that customer service or helpdesk staff that an organization provides or uses can recognise an incident and know how to contact the relevant data processor for advice.

There are a number of providers of these courses, both classroom-based and online, so the customer organization can choose that course that best fits with the requirements and preferred mode of delivery. It can safely be said that courses relating to this certification are not so technically demanding as those delivered under the CREST scheme.

Team Training

Training that rehearses teams in the procedures and processes that are required in dealing with a significant incident can be very valuable. Any organization that is significantly large or carries out critical functions needs to ensure that the team tasked with dealing with such events efficiently and analysing their actions after the event and needs to learn to do that in the safe environment of a training event. If the head of incident response has a lot of experience, they may feel that they have the competence to run such exercises internally. However, it is always worth considering using a quality external training provider at least once to give an impartial perspective.

It is always a good idea to consider recommendations, especially where a course is expensive. Let's face it – Amazon's use of customer reviews appears to have had a significant impact on how we consider how we spend our money as private citizens. Just yesterday, I caught myself carefully reading the range of reviews for a book I was considering, and the book only cost £15. How much more careful should an organization be when it comes to spending significant amounts of the company's training money? Any good training company should be able to give you references from past attendees. Of course, these are likely to be biased towards those who liked the course, but they will help to understand the required background knowledge that is helpful and the mode of delivery that was effective and why.

Revealing the Case Studies

Amber Inc.

The clear issue with Amber Inc. is that there is nobody in the organization who has information (or cyber, come to that) security formal knowledge or training. It is clear that they have some knowledge regarding IT security, but this is not wide enough to give them help in the wider area of incident response. As in any situation, there is a budget concern regarding security training; how much they need and who needs it. However, the external pressure for compliance with ISO 27001 means they need to be able to demonstrate that the senior levels of the organization take security seriously. One way to do this is to invest in some training, but given the problems such as time required, which is of even greater importance when staff are seconded in from another team, the training must be carefully selected.

One exercise is to look at those incidents that have occurred, the opinion of those involved and see where specific training might have helped the handling. It is also important to look for situations where formal training of a small number of staff could allow such learning to be cascaded to other staff when required.

In the first instance, it is most effective for training that is a development of knowledge that staff already have, so in this case, that would be technical knowledge and experience. It is advisable though, that the IR manager be vigilant against any training gaps that are uncovered in post-incident reviews, especially if any members of staff express an interest in developing their skills in that area.

As the organization develops towards accreditation then advice can be taken from the person, or organization who is assisting their preparation as their experience as well as a less partial, external view of Amber Inc.'s situation would help training budget decisions.

Jade Ltd.

Staff training is a big issue for Jade Ltd., as they have no specialist security staff and no security awareness program. This means they really have two distinct training requirements. There is the need to increase awareness of all staff, most especially those handling sensitive information or dealing with customer queries. They also need to develop a body of understanding and competence in the handling of security incidents.

As they are recruiting an experienced incident manager, one of their initial tasks should include identifying the existing knowledge of staff who would be working in the IR team. Examination of existing incident reports from the last year may well indicate areas where training of one or two staff members in specific skills and knowledge would benefit the IR function.

The second part of the training challenge is with regard to security awareness of all staff. This is a surprisingly tricky area to select the appropriate training for, not least because awareness is such a broad, soft skill to train in. It is important, therefore, that the new IR manager brings together the opinions of relevant senior managers together with a representative of the HR and, if they have one, training, functional areas. They should be able to identify training techniques that work or don't work within the existing organizational culture. It is also useful to identify the key messages that they feel are a priority to instill in the staff and decide how success in communicating these messages is to be measured. With awareness this can be hard, but the real world of business requires that return on investment needs to be demonstrated, and that applies to training, too. However, a word of caution: Don't go for a particular method of communication just because it is easier to measure success, as this may not be the best way to get actual behaviour change. For example, while Computer-Based Training (CBT) is very powerful in generating information regarding the progress of staff understanding, the rate of transfer of that understanding into a change behaviour is generally less reliable. If CBT is used, it is often best to combine with some other motivation if a change in action is required. For example, staff may understand that wearing their ID badges when they go outside the office might draw the attention of someone who might be interested in the contents of their phone or other device that they are carrying. However, when they are "just nipping out to get a sandwich," they may not think that the risk is strong enough to make them put the badges in a pocket or bag. However, a system of fines (collected for a local charity) for any who are seen outside wearing their badge might motivate their change of action.

As with Amber Inc., the progress of any training, especially specialist training for IR team members, should fit either with the ongoing challenges the IR face, and requirements that experienced staff, in this case primarily the IR manager, may identify.

16

MANAGING THE INVESTIGATIONS CYCLE

Notification, Reporting and Expectancy Management

I was aware. That is I became aware. Slowly. Gradually. I could hardly help it, could I? When the same thing kept happening, over and over and over and over again! Every life I ever lived, I got killed by Arthur Dent.

Douglas Adams
Hitchhikers Guide to the Galaxy, the Tertiary Stage

Information in this chapter:

- Your priorities
- "The White Team"
- Expectancy management
- Notification and reporting
- The investigations cycle itself
- Closing time

Introduction

We have covered the cyclic model of investigations in the first part of the book and in more detail in Chapter 8. However, effective in order to effectively manage within a theoretical model it is an effective manager must be able to identify those things which are directly critical to the investigation handling, and those where they should be directing and monitoring rather than actively participating.

The IR manager should also be aware of managing the human aspects requirements of the team in order to effectively develop and maintain it. This is discussed in the next chapter.

The tasks that will most likely stick to your desk in an incident include liaison with your management, with external agencies (covered in Chapter 14), task direction and prioritisation, notification and reporting.

You may also be involved in the preparation for and management of meetings, whether these be face to face, telephone, virtual or, in all unfortunate probability, mixed.

Your Priorities

With so many different elements being present in most incidents, prioritization of management time and attention is vital. A key priority of the incident manager is to ensure that they are aware of any core material changes, especially where they might impact how it is handled. For example, "Are we still dealing with what we thought we were dealing with?" To give a trivial example; an investigation into email harassment, while it is significant of itself may uncover evidence of different, or more serious, misconduct. This is depressingly common, so it can often seem that people tempted to do wrong in one part of their work don't limit their misdemeanour to one act.

As incident manager, you should expect to be in regular if not continuous communication with the business and, except for trivial incidents, with the executive. Their requirements and priorities may change; you need to realise the impact that this has on the current incident activities and amend those at the earliest reasonable opportunity.

There will also be specific activities that fall to you as the incident manager. We have already mentioned notification and reporting, but a critical aspect of perceived success or failure in incident handling is expectancy management.

The White Team

The upper management of any incident are those people who set requirements and priorities of the incident handling and management. These are often referred to as "The White Team." In a small or medium-sized organization, this may comprise of one senior representative of the business with yourself and some additional advisors, for example, HR, Communications or Legal. In larger organizations, this may be a significant group of people, quite often with conflicting responsibilities and therefore, requirements. Obviously, the White Team are one of the first groups who need to be notified that an incident is underway and may be the first group to which you have to present some sort of formal report. Often, the team will have minimal experience of information or cyber security issues, frustratingly often are unaware of any legal or regulatory reporting requirements, and the restrictions those bring on your freedom of action. Frankly, it is your job to keep them informed, guided and under control or, in the worst cases, away from communicating and disturbing the investigations team. They are probably the most significant focus of your expectancy management activities.

Expectancy Management

It is rare that at the start of an incident, it is possible to accurately predict how long something is actually going to take. It should be said that throughout your career in IR it is to be expected that you will continue to be surprised just what strange results can ensue from what you thought was a straightforward task. While you are busy doing your bit, other people outside your team will be relaying on you for necessary inputs to their activities. They may have had to promise to key stakeholders, or external bodies, certain actions will be complete by a fixed timeframe. For example, under GDPR, initial incident reports must be with the national supervisory authority within 72 hours. Depending on your jurisdiction, other law or regulation may determine other time scales or promises, which may have been given on the basis of a more, or less informed estimate (aka guess). As noted above, one area where you have responsibility is to help ensure any such "estimates" are as reasonable as you can currently make them.

However, things change, computers go wrong, people make mistakes and new and higher priority issues may interfere. It is therefore important that you are aware of what others are relaying on, and be able to inform them appropriately whenever anything changes that will affect them and ideally before their deadlines expire.

For these reasons, it is vital that you keep a constant eye on progress, and not limit it to specific points in the cycle. Where you are not sure about a potential impact to a promised delivery, it is always worth discussing it early to allow other people to re-plan their actions just as you are likely to be re-planning yours.

Notification and Reporting

There are a wide range of agencies with whom you will need to communicate on a relatively formal basis. As well as the White Team and data protection regulators, it may be expedient to alert your ISP so they can take steps to retain more detailed log information. It may also be important to be aware that in some circumstances and jurisdictions there is a responsibility, or even requirement, to report certain incident types to legal and other regulatory authorities.

Press statements and customer communications should be handled by the appropriate trained personnel, but it is wise to ensure that these are up to date and, ideally, statements are checked for technical accuracy prior to are release.

Generally, these communications split into two broad groups: notifications and reports. Notifications are a brief statement of an incident, possibly with a time line for the next expected communication. Reports are usually significantly longer and more detailed.

You should be getting notifications and reports from your team and collaborating investigators. If you are exceptionally lucky you may be able to simply pass these on to appropriate stakeholders, but they will often require to be précised or to be rewritten in less technical language.

It is well worth keeping a detailed timeline of when notifications, reports and updates are due, whether or not you are the expected author, so that you can ensure sufficient task time is made available for adequate preparation.

The Investigations Cycle Itself

Managing the Incident Meetings

Hopefully, you are an experienced enough manager (or, indeed, executive) to have no problem in running a meeting. You will be aware that preparation is often the key to a good meeting. The agenda should be flexible enough and properly updated before the meeting starts that "any other (competent) business" does not become the majority of the meeting. If those attending the meeting are strongly encouraged to pre-read discussion documents, this can cut down on the time required, and control that needs to be exercised by the chair to ensure proper timekeeping. Even practices such as the "stand-up meeting" to keep meetings short may be used, depending on your organizational culture.

However, in many incident response scenarios, you will not have the advantage of preparation, not least because there is little chance to circulate documents prior to the meeting,* and you are unlikely to have a meeting secretary.

Determining how tight the investigations cycle should be is going to be vital to the success of the management of the incident. If you are trying to cram everything, that is meeting and actions, into an hour, there will be very little time available to actually accomplish or even substantively progress the ongoing activities. However, pushing the cycle out to a fortnight stakeholders would lead stakeholders to the conclusion that handling the incident it is not an organizational priority. Somewhere in the middle lies a happy medium.

Often, an incident will start off with quite a tight cycle, this being able to be relaxed as the information about the incident emerges. At that point, it will be possible to have clearer timescales for completion of the various activities.

It is important that the number and duration of incident meetings is set so that as incident manager you can attend most of them, not least to and ensure that everybody keeps to time. In small organizations or simple incidents (simple should not be read as implying trivial), you may be able to get away with just one meeting. However, once the number of participants gets above 10–12, especially if many or all are connecting remotely, this becomes very difficult to handle and you may need to reconsider your approach. For example, less frequent but regular update meetings for the White Team may be acceptable. Equally, if investigations and rectification activities are now following independent paths, it may be sensible to split these into two meetings although you should ensure that suitable, usually management,

---

* And everybody, except Audit, if you have been forced to let them in, will have been too busy to give them more than a cursory glance.

cross-representation happens in case specific proposed activities could cause conflict with the other area.

While control of the agenda is vital, equally important is the competence of the meeting chair. They should be able to limit the digression off pertinent topic, while still ensuring that all stakeholder areas are given opportunity to contribute. Particularly in significant incidents, it is often difficult for more junior staff to believe that their input will be welcome. However, they are often the people "at the coal face" of technical support and direct customer interaction and therefore could have important information to share. Also, in our experience, they tend to be the people with the fewest fixed ideas about "what an incident should be like."

As noted above, you, as incident manager, will often be the person with the strongest grasp on business requirements and priorities, how these interact with the existing ongoing actions and what modifications or additional activities might be required to accommodate changes. Where the latter are significant, you may wish to break reporting of these activities out of the current cycle and hold the appropriate meetings in the right order, to discuss, confirm and commence the right actions.

A Short Meeting

In the early stages of any incident, the primary object of a meeting is to get all operational team members back to working on the incident, while still allowing you to take proper notice of any changes in the business requirement, the circumstances of the incident or the resources available.

Firstly, make sure that where possible, any documentation produced is discussed prior to the meeting so that relevant options, or if it is within your comfort zone, your fait accompli, can be presented.

The meeting should follow something like this basic agenda:

- Does anybody* have new information that suggests we may be doing the wrong things?

---

* We have found it to be useful to make it compulsory for all attendees to contribute at this point. Especially if you have relatively inexperienced team members, this can be a useful tool to make sure they feel that they are allowed to contribute.

- An update from you on any direction from higher management on the business requirements or reports down from higher-level meetings.
- Very brief updates on current actions – these should be limited to:
  - Complete
  - Ongoing according to plan
  - Ongoing but delayed
  - Stalled
  - Not yet started
- Lead a review of any new actions required and any reprioritisation of existing actions.
- Assignment of resources to the actions.
- Time of next meeting.

If You Have the Time

Generally, there is a useful structure to the meeting and some of it is very similar:

1. Is there anything urgent somebody needs to bring up that might mean the meeting should be postponed or repurposed to deal with it?
2. Status on progress on actions from the last meeting. Make this very brief to start with, using something similar to the short meeting report.
3. Where any aspect of this is a surprise or of concern to you, you can then go back to the teams or individuals for a more detailed report.
4. *New information*: This is the meat of the meeting. Is there any new information, as a result of team activities or from elsewhere, that might change your perception of the situation? If the information is unclear or from a source of dubious reliability but would be material to your understanding of the incident if correct, then you have some confirmatory activities for somebody to undertake.
5. *New direction or advice*: Changes in business requirements or advice from legal or other sources will affect your actions.

6. New actions or proposed modifications to existing actions. This should be a bit of a round-table exercise, allowing suggestions from all present, if you have time but culminating in the incident manager proposing a course of action and having this approved by the senior business representative.

7. *Allocation of actions*: Depending on how radical the changes agreed were, this may require re-tasking of teams. Where people do not have any obvious actions assignable – do they have secondary skills which could assist another team or aspect of the investigation?

8. That would normally conclude the formal meeting – although "Any Other Business" will usually be called, the team should be encourage to bring up any aspects in the relevant main section.

9. Longer reports can now be taken with only the relevant people attending and most away back at work. If necessary, critical aspects can be briefed in to, or the reports made available prior to, the next meeting.

Setting SMART Tasks

When you are setting tasks of whichever type, it is useful to remember, if not to be bound by, the "SMART Objectives criteria."*

- Specific – Or Simple. Quite a lot of the time, your team will be having to liaise with people who have no experience of incident management. This makes it important that tasks are described ideally in plain, non-technical language or, if absolutely necessary, common IT jargon. It is important to appreciate that people are likely to become tired and stressed. The more guidance you can give them when setting the task, the better they are likely to achieve it.†

---

* If this particular bit of management speak has eluded you, then the Wikipedia page "SMART criteria" is a very good primer. Please note, for the more technical reader, that I am not, in any way, referring to "Self-Monitoring, Analysis, and Reporting Technology" as available on some hard disk drives near you. Other storage devices, as well as other management fads, are available!

† Although this does need to be balanced against being patronizing to the more experienced of your team. In that case, you might set them the task in general terms and then get them to split it for you in to simpler component task elements, either as part of the meeting or immediately afterwards (but still forming part of the meeting record.)

- "Who" – You need to detail off the resources that you are employing on this task – personnel and technical.
- "What" – They need to know what you intend them to achieve.*
- "Why" – Usually, if your team are reasonably experienced, the "Why?" element will either be blatantly obvious or generally accepted in an ongoing incident. Of course, it may be necessary to give guidance to newer team members or secondees. In invasive investigations, that may compromise peoples' privacy and so the "why" might formally refer to the required detailed justification for the privacy breach by relevant legal or regulatory authorities.
- "When" – When a time for something to be required isn't immediately (and it often is), this needs to be both spelt out and for purposes of expectancy management (theirs, yours and your managements), recorded. Often, you will have activities that will need to wait until the start of working hours, which may be either in your location or if you need to contact, say, a hosting company or a registrar, in a foreign location.
- "Where" – Where the receiver of the information it isn't obvious, this may also need to be detailed. Remember that people may not be operating at their best and, provided you can keep it from becoming, or feeling, like a personal pressure on themselves by directing contact through yourself. The team knows that you will be reporting upwards, if not also sideways, therefore asking them to make sure that information is SMART, but having you check it before pushing it to the person requiring it can take some of the stress off. Making the target for information specific rather than vague is important so it is important to ensure contact details for those who may be involved in an incident, either operationally, or as a stakeholder, kept up to date. In the IM context, one vital aspect of "where" are

---

* This is, of course, particularly important if you are sending somebody to the coffee shop!

contact details, both for the team and for those they will be liaising or working with.

- Measurable – The team (and you) need to have a fairly clear idea what success looks like for each task or element thereof. That way, they know when they can stop and return to being an available resource for you for the next part of the job.

- Achievable (also Realistic, although that is sometimes used below) – Simply enough, you need to ensure that not only is what you are doing correct and reasonable, but it should be achievable. This may seem obvious, but it is a trap, especially for inexperienced teams.

- Relevant – What is being done should be recognizable as relevant to the overall achievement of one or more of the business requirements. Admittedly, you may find yourself needing to undertake some activities to appease management (who do have their fads and foibles) but try to leave those, if you can, until a relatively quiet time in the overall cycle.*

- Time-Bound – Regardless of whether the task is immediate or for some reason delayed, it should be something that can be significantly progressed, if not completed, in a small multiple of the time interval between your progress review meetings. Again, where this is impractical (a complex task may actually be best handled by one person or a small team, who are given a high degree of freedom of action), a task may be best split into elements with a shorter time to fruition.

Being Aware of Your Team

Because of the nature of the formal meetings, it is well worth using some of the limited spare time you will have between meetings,

---

* Cynically, if they really are demanding nugatory effort and cannot be deflect, you could always employ the tactic made infamous by Sir Robert Armstrong, then the British Cabinet Secretary and now Baron Armstrong of Ilminster and be "economical with the truth." That may, of course, not be a wise or (career) safe course of action.

reporting, and other essential administration to discuss things less formally with the teams tasked to individual activities. This is where you are likely to get the earliest warning of material changes to incident information and potential delays in the completion of activities.

It also allows you to keep an eye on the human tendency to work towards their own strengths. One of Matthew's investigators was an email expert, having run an email support team, and having extensive experience of using email in the investigation of incidents. Unfortunately, when he was first becoming involved in wider and more technically challenging investigations, he had a habit of deciding that the critical activity must involve investigation of one or more people's email accounts. It took him a while to overcome this. Equally, network engineers have a tendency to look at network component logs, web developers to website vulnerabilities and exploits and we are sure you will be able to supply other examples. As you are largely going to have to trust your teams to get on with things themselves, it is necessary to keep some degree of eye on them at this high level.

You may be in the situation where privileged access is quite granular and needs to be authorised on a case-by-case basis, so you will be notified if a member or a team is going "off piste." Do not be too quick to stop them, however. Check why they are thinking along those lines because they may have come across some new information that honestly does point at their preferred direction being sensible.

Closing Time?

The incident manager having an overall view of the incident is likely to be the first to see when it is approaching time to formally close the incident. As activities complete, no new business requirements appear, and new information becomes sparse or trivial, you will want to move back to "BAU"* working.

Especially with larger, more complex or more sensitive incidents, closing should be discussed with the White Team if a meeting with them has been called, and with other relevant stakeholders.

Remember that you will need to secure all of the incident and investigations data for the post-incident review.

---

* Business As Usual.

Revealing the Case Studies

Amber Inc.

With Amber Inc., the IR team is built around the IT team. This means that incorporating the skills of other departments such as customer service and those with responsibility for contact with the media may not be considered in the early days of developing the IR team. When the team runs training and table-top exercises, it is important that the most likely contacts within relevant associate teams are included. It needs to be appreciated in the design of the investigations cycle that some of this associate teams may slow the process down by wanting more information or wanting to consult with an external expert before a decision is made. For example, a HR team member may want to consult a member of the internal or external legal resource before proceeding in an incident that has repercussions for the HR function. Of course, the fact that Amber Inc. is a multinational organization means that local legal and regulatory requirements on the incident handling process may need to be checked. It is important that this is understood as early as possible so these contributions, where they make a positive contribution to the handling of the incident, are not seen as getting in the way of effective incident response.

Even if associate teams are not involved in every exercise, they can often contribute useful observations and insights. They may also be able to explain how they could contribute to the handling of an incident that was not expected to require their input.

All of these findings demonstrate the utility of regular and effective training, including table-top workshops, for all who may be involved in incident response handling.

Jade Ltd.

Those who have incident response for Jade Ltd. as part or all of their job specification should be aware of the critical concern that would be likely to arise as a result of any incident that was likely to expose information they process. The impact on the investigations cycle is likely to be that the number of stakeholders who require to be kept fully informed is higher than would be expected for other organizations of a similar size. This puts the management of communication, including meetings, as a core contributor to the success of the handling of an incident.

Because the stakeholders will include external regulators who have a legal requirement to be kept informed in the case of risk to sensitive information, these requirements need to be fully understood and incorporated into the investigations cycle to significantly reduce the likelihood of the fallout from a significant incident to include externally enforced penalties, and the publicity that go with them.

Another result of the nature of the information they process is that incidents and potential incidents need to be recognised early and flagged to the IR team. This means that many more staff than those who will play an active part in the investigation process, must be able to demonstrate a clear understanding of the symptoms that might indicate an issue.

A particular concern would be in the reporting by someone who believes they have either taken some action that may have exposed data or feel that they would be likely to be blamed for doing so. A key question in the design of any behaviour model is "why should they do that?" It is easy to see that in this sort of situation it is important that there be a positive, or at the very least, a neutral reflection on them. Like honesty in the post-incident review process, designing a first notification process that does not penalize the reporter is not easy. However, it is something that would balance out in the increase in the willingness to report incidents to which they have contributed. There is no "one-size-fits-all" answer to this problem. It will need to fit with the organizational culture. Using the organizational approach to whistle-blowing or the reporting of bullying may give present a starting point.

17
TEAM MANAGEMENT

Now this is a very difficult job and the only way to get through it is we all work together as a team. And that means you do everything I say.

Sir Michael Cain
The Italian Job (1969)

Information in this chapter:

- Incident assignment
- Continuity versus fatigue
- Managing your contacts
- Managing handovers
- Working with ITIL – Incident & problem management

Introduction

Effective team management challenging can sometimes feel like a two-level game of plate spinning. The manager is holding plates with his staff spinning on them and they, in turn, are minding any number of spinning plates. When it goes well, it goes really well, but if the set up or operation is sub-optimal, then the additional pressure of incident response can make the situation precarious.

Incident Assignment

One of the interesting discussions we had in the composition of this book was with regard to the approach to the management of an IR team in their day to day work, and the management of specific incidents, especially where they include high pressure situations. Both aspects of their work are important, but they can require significantly different approaches. Where the internal team is of a reasonable size and contains a range of skills and experience, the manager needs to be aware of range of ability and potential. While this can be challenging in terms of tracking training and feedback from incidents, it is not that which makes it significantly more challenging than many other situations. The particular problem comes from the sometimes politically sensitive nature of incidents and post incident reviews which can make it harder for staff to indicate their own weaknesses and personal development concerns.

There are other concerns, especially if an incident might mean out of hours working. In Chapter 13, background and family issues which might impact out-of-hours working are discussed. It is worth appreciating that there are also personal issues, such as a person's religious practices or medical or requirements or limitations that need to be considered. In mentioning this very sensitive area, I do not include whether a team member might have strong objections to dealing with particular types of incident, such as those relating to the transmission or sharing of indecent images within the organization, as has been discussed in Chapter 10. This is best addressed at the pre-employment stage. In the operational context of this chapter, the particular concern is where staff are firm adherents to a Holy day within the week. As this will be a consistent issue and so is one that guides the development of schedules. It is important that a team member should not be made to feel that their adherence is not respected. Some staff may find their religious community is part of their wider support network, especially if they do have to deal with incidents that might cause them distress. The incident manager therefore should find benefit for the whole team in incorporating Holy days into the schedule in discussion with the team member themselves.

Continuity versus Fatigue

Generally, during an incident you are going to want to maintain continuity of personnel. Knowledge of that specific incident, especially any quirks that differentiate it from similar incidents, is often vital to finding an efficient solution. However, we also need to consider the realities of human behaviour. As fatigue sets in, although people can maintain a reasonable competence in the performance of basic or well-understood tasks, their ability to reason at a higher level often reduces.

Not all incidents will be fundamentally time pressured in the way the team handle them. Some time factors will be outside the team's control, such as forensic activity or restoration from back up. Others may be fundamentally operating at business, rather than technical timescales such as an internal disciplinary. In cases like these, fatigue management is easy. Staff can be sent home to get a good meal and catch up on rest while issues continue to resolve.

However, it is more common for incident response to be fundamentally time pressured. Packing up and going home in the middle of DDoS attack against your main transactional website is unlikely to endear you to the business function, however much it may be a welcome relief for your team. Obviously, if suitable alternative staff are available, a properly engineered hand-over to a fresh set of investigators is likely to restore some degree of effectiveness. Otherwise, it may be necessary to cycle your team through rest and limit their tasks to those they best understand until you have a fully capable team back. Obviously, if this continues for several days additional support from ICT, and your partners, may be essential. It is also quite useful to make careful notes of these events as evidence for future budget and team sizing negotiations.

Having dealt with your team, now all you need to worry about it your own capabilities. One of the things that deteriorate quite quickly when they are working a long or complicated incident is a person's ability to cope with inconsistency. During a significant incident, an IR manager can be expected to maintain the consistency between what is actually going on, the executives' understanding of what is going on, as well being mindful of the tension between the business's desired intermediate and end states and the necessary investigative and technical tasks. It is no surprise therefore, that they find a reduction in their ability to maintain the balance between these demands as they become tired. As IR needs to function as an inclusive team, so they can play a part in ensuring the manager remains effective. They can point out those warning signs to a fall off in quality of function or just effective interaction that they may not have recognised in themselves. How rest or replacement of the IR manager or leader will very much depend on the organization and its culture, but it needs to be prepared for and handled properly or else the overall incident management is likely to materially suffer.

Managing Contacts

Whatever the size of the business and its incident response team there will be a need to interact with external people and agencies. If the incident response team is small and supported by links with external specialists such as computer forensics consultants, the manager needs to ensure that the flow of effective feedback both from those consultants and from staff on how the consultant worked with the team. As we discussed above, situations where external consultants are called in are likely to be infrequent,* so it is important that effort to keep the contact "warm" in terms of their relationship with the team. This can really pay dividends in terms of their ability to hit the ground running as they understand their role in a fast moving incident. If, for example, there have been significant changes to the organizational infrastructure, then any network engineering or forensics support external consultants will need detailed knowledge of the changes in order to be effective. If this is not provided in advance, then time will be lost while they try to catch up or make guesses based on current understanding.

Obviously, maintaining an up to date list of contacts in key suppliers and other partner organizations, specialists advisers, for example legal, and if it is permitted, regulatory and law enforcement bodies is essential. It also helps if these people have a reasonable awareness of who you and your team are, this means liaison and update meetings are a critical part of the IR manager's role. To put it another way, if an important call to one of these key contacts has to be made at three o'clock on a Sunday morning, it is often useful for them to remember that you bought lunch (if such a thing is permitted by your organizations' policy) or that they have some trust that the IR function is unlikely to be calling un-necessarily. Obviously there needs to be an up to date list of external contacts out of hours contact details.

Some contacts will be more role-based rather than personal. The duty manager at a backup storage location simply needs the right authorisation to realise the required tape or other device. However, the process for enacting authorisation needs to be clearly understood both by those required to authorise, as well those at the data centre who need to ratify that authority. Equally, if the response from them

---

* Or else you would be considering providing some sort of internal provision.

has certain limitations, for example the storage facility is four hours travel from your site, you need to be aware of this so you can factor it into your expectancy management calculations.

As an incident progresses, it is important to understand that many of the contacts may be on a more normal business hours schedule than you are, or work shifts. Understanding their availability and their hand-overs will help to prevent you from missing a limitation and promising things that cannot be delivered.

Of specific importance is to note any changes in the most appropriate contact compared to the lists in your incident management documentation. Job moves, re-organizations and other staff changes are just as likely to happen in the organizations you depend upon as they are in your own.

Managing Handovers

Handovers are the norm in any organization that requires shift work were jobs are ongoing. Remembering the unofficial title for this book *Incident Management for the Tired and Confused,* especially if an incident is handing over after a period of intense work, it is probable that the member of staff who is handing over is very tired and may not remember all aspects of the incident. Any complex incident needs careful record keeping, and it worth remembering that not all complex incidents appear so at the beginning.

When an incident is active across the duty time of more than one person it leaves open a potential weakness in the handling of the situation because, by the nature of the event the incoming duty person has not experienced the events immediately preceding their take over. Actions or processes may be assumed to have happened and new information may be missed. Therefore, where hand-overs may be required they need to be properly planned and use a standard framework procedure particularly for hand-overs between incident managers and between lead investigators. These procedures cannot be too prescriptive or else they will not be sufficiently flexible to deal with the differing context of various incidents. Indeed, it is unlikely that any two incidents, even involving a similar threat or issue, will be the same. If there is a continuity member, that is a member of the team that works across the formal handover, whether at the same or a different level, it is also worth including them as they can help to maintain a consistent approach.

If we consider the two extremes of intensity of action during an incident there is the situation where things are changing quickly and decisions are required on a regular basis. On the other hand, there are the incidents that are winding down or were not very complex anyway. Obviously, the critical situation where things are intense and fast moving is the most critical to hand over effectively, but actually both need to be covering similar information, not least to ensure that the process becomes very familiar to staff, even when they are very tired and unmotivated by events. So, the incoming duty person needs to know something of each of the following:

- What happened – the background.
- What is happening – at the point of handover.
- What should be happening – waiting for information or action from others.
- What has **changed** since the last time that person was involved with this incident.

If the incident is not fast-moving, then there probably would be chance for the incoming person to familiarize themselves with all the information that they have been given, but, especially if they have already worked on the incident, they shouldn't have to. The critical question of those four questions indicates the key to the effective hand-over. Especially if the incoming duty person was involved in the incident earlier on, what they critically need to know is what has changed since they were last involved. This cuts across background and information that they may have provided into the records earlier and gives them the developments that they need to be aware of.

Additionally, it's important to ensure that the IR manager has taken adequate personal notes, as well as the formal incident record and that these are current. Obviously, this importance can be raised to critical if the incident is complex, unusual or if there are manning or communication issues between various imputing personnel. Depending on the level that is being handed over, the content of notes will vary, but they should describe current active tasks, tasks that have been paused for whatever reason and any material changes in the context of or your understanding of the incident since the person you are handing over to was last involved. Obviously, if the person in receipt of these notes has no experience of this particular incident type before, then the hand-over will need to be significantly more comprehensive than if they were returning from, say, a 12-hour stand-down or they have plenty of experience of this sort of event.

Particularly for investigator hand-overs, you also need to be aware of any jurisdictional requirements for chain or custody of evidence. This may require physical sighting of stored artefacts, corroborative signatures in investigative notebooks, or similar formal steps. This is something that has to be done correctly, especially if action is to be taken based on evidence collected.

A Final Note

Overall, it is the responsibility of the IR manager to look out for the welfare of their team and themselves. Exhausted people may be capable of brilliant work, but it is much less likely than when they are properly rested. This can be as simple as bringing in a favourite take-away food to support late evening working or managing a process of regular shift hangovers.

Revealing the Case Studies

Amber Inc.

The advantage this team has is that its head has experience. What they may find difficult to begin with is that they are used to a dedicated team who have worked together for a reasonably long time. A team who have experience of a wide range of incidents, not just IT, and an understanding of the various skills that are needed in an IM team. They may find it difficult to think about such basic elements of the IM process as it will have been a well-practiced routine. It's similar to the situation where a person has been driving a car solely in the UK for many years, and they then find they need to drive in a country where they drive on the right hand side of the road. The change is not just a matter of remembering to stay on the right side, it involves manoeuvres around roundabouts, looking for oncoming traffic when joining a new road, who to give way to in narrow streets and what to do when an emergency vehicle is baring down with lights and sirens indicating the need for instant action. All of these are changes that will need to be considered and are simply not covered by "just drive on the side that has you next to the curb." The IM head is going to need to ensure his staff notice everything about an incident, record it and hand it over effectively, with all the detail that the incoming duty person needs to handle the situation, not more and certainly not less.

Jade Ltd.

Jade Ltd. is just developing its incident management function so many of the more complex skills, such as legal advice and off site data storage are drawn into incidents when required. This makes it even more important that good records are kept, and that the person taking on the duty has the support that they feel they need. For example, the IM head may have been taking the duty role from the start of an incident on Friday night until Sunday evening. They will know the person they are handing on to, because of their managerial role, and will therefore need to find support for any weak areas of the duty person's skill or experience set that is likely to be required. Other members who provide duty cover to the team, who may not know as much about their incoming colleague will rely on that colleague making that assessment for themselves, and that can be difficult.

Also in this situation, contact with relevant external specialists needs to be logged and notified in the hand-over. If the external consultant is contacted, the nature of the support they can provide discussed and necessary decisions then taken, it is important that the incoming duty person doesn't miss that contact and move to have the same discussion again. Especially if this is at antisocial hours, this is likely to slightly sour relations and potentially cost the company for the extra discussion.

18

RECORDING INFORMATION, ACTIVITIES AND DECISIONS

Here Bilbo's hand ended and Frodo had written "The downfall of the Lord of the Rings and the Return of the King". 'Why, you have nearly finished it Mr Frodo!' Sam exclaimed. 'Well you have kept at it, I must say.' 'I have quite finished, Sam,' said Frodo. 'The last pages are for you'.

J. R. R. Tolkien
The Lord of the Rings

Introduction

In Chapter 17, there was mention of the importance of the notes of the incident manager in the context of handovers for incidents that take longer than the time one manager can reasonably remain in control without a break and rest. This chapter develops that need for data and action recording. While an IR function is in its early days the ability to be able to reflect on how incidents are handled in some detail, is especially important.

While the incident is progressing, it is essential to record a significant amount of information regarding the development of the incident and the progress of any investigations and recovery activities. This may seem to be common sense, but in the middle of an incident, especially one that is very intensive, making contemporaneous notes can be put off, or forgotten until a point when the exact requests, actions and reasons behind them can have become less clear.

Exactly how and where information should be recorded will vary between organisations, but it may be worth considering making paper or offline notes in the first instance in case, in the course of the incident handling, any online system is shut down. Losing access to information such as who was to do what and why might have a significant impact on the restoration of their system.

There also needs to be guidance for the incident response team as to what information needs to be captured, recorded or otherwise attached to the incident. It is essential that these meet any legal and regulatory requirements for such incidents. For example, if photographic or other material that is considered illegal precise details regarding its handling, and contact made with the appropriate lawful authorities, and detail of any requests or advice they give must be recorded with care as mishandling could hamper any prosecution that might be otherwise pursued.

It is also important to remember any regulatory requirements you might have for recording specific items or classes of information. Breach notification requirements – whether to regulators or affected data subjects, or both – may require you to spend time recording detailed information rather than conducting further investigations activities. The short (72-hour) notification requirement with the EU General Data Protection Regulation may very well, for those affected (which will include any organisation with EU residents affected by a breach, regardless of your own jurisdiction), significantly impact on your ability to conduct investigative and restorative work.

Basic Records

Incident Metadata

You need to be able to record ownership and audit data for incidents. At a minimum, this should include:

- A unique incident number.
- Authorisation for the incident to be pursued.
- Incident categorisation.
- Current and previous incident priorities, with times and reasons for changes.
- Contact details for the current incident management team.
- Reference details of any personal data subjects affected by the breach.

For larger organisations, you may have to record significantly more information. This might include:

- Resources expended
  - Incident team time.*
  - Any expenditure, including replacement of consumable items.
- Contact details for members from the wider incident team (e.g. legal, public relations, etc.).
- Transfers of authority between incident managers or between service, security and BCP/DR incident processes.
- Advice or reports received from internal or external partners.

Initiation

First, it is essential to record the initiation of the incident. Investigations are likely to have business or privacy impact, or both, so the initial authority to conduct the investigation must be recorded. Depending on the delegated authority, this may be done by the incident helpdesk, the on-duty incident manager or a more senior manager. Different types of incidents may require authorisation at different levels.

Incident Narrative

During the incident progress, important new information or evidence, key decisions and significant reports should be logged and, where appropriate, commented on by the incident manager.

The recording of this information is essential to allow a proper post-incident review. In many cases, the most important thing for a PIR to consider is the understanding of the current of the current at of the incident by the key participants, and how that agrees or conflicts with their objective review, based both on the information available at the time and of their probably better informed hindsight, as this may take place some time after the main investigative and restoration activities, when details are no longer at the forefront of the participants' memories. We will look at that in more detail in the next chapter.

For incidents, it also *enables* handovers where the rate of work in the incident requires shift working.

---

* If you are fortunate enough to be running an overtime system, this can be used to produce automated reports for HR.

Incident Summary

It is very useful, albeit not essential, for the incident manager to maintain a current summary, no more than a couple of short paragraphs, of the status of the incident. This is extremely useful for oncoming shift briefings and composite management reports.

Each incident manager will develop their own style and this should reflect the requirements of the audience of this section. If you have a well-engineered and dedicated incident reporting system, it is this this summery paragraph in addition to relevant meta data that you might wish to make available to the "read-only" user community. Elements that should be considered for inclusion are:

- Any changes in business priority.
- Investigation or recovery activities and any mother material changes in your view of the incident.
- Hand overs between team members with specific authority such as between incident managers should also be noted here as well as the formal record in the narrative.

A particularly critical example is the closure report. This should address when, why and whose authority the incident was closed, and include copies of, or links to final versions of ALL pertinent reports. You will probably wish to establish at least a semi-formalized template for this report, given its significance in the overall process.

Approval of Privilege Use

Both investigations and recovery action are likely to require the use of privileges in excess of those normally allocated to the technicians. Approval for use of super-user and similar privileges, as well as any privileges to complete emergency changes, should be recorded to ensure an appropriate audit trail. Equally, when the use of privileges is relinquished, either because the situation has changed or because the activities are complete, this should be recorded. In critical emergency situations, it may be necessary to alter the ICT state so quickly that it is not possible to follow the full change control process. Obviously, a full explanation of the situation leading to this will need to be recorded as contemporaneously as possible in order that it can be analysed at the post-incident review.

Reports and Notes

The issuing of briefing notes, management reports and similar products should be recorded. If possible, the actual files should be stored as part of the investigations record. At a minimum, the date and time of issue a link to the document/s within your information management file storage system and the distribution list should be recorded.

Where the incident manager receives significant reports, whether from investigators, external specialists or other information sources (such as vendor announcements of a vulnerability pertinent to the incident) or reports on the malware you are dealing with, these should be included in the same way. If your system does not display these competently to the active participants, you may also wish to distribute them by email or other route ensuring important information is highlighted to relevant parties.

Task Tracker

If practical, a task tracker with assigned staff and tracking dates or times should be added. This can report per incident, by staff member and as an overall list of outstanding items.

Post-Incident Review

If a task management system is implemented, it is worth having a "post-incident review" task automatically created whenever a task is formally closed and assigned, initially, to the senior incident manager. A due date should be assigned – not immediately – to allow the involved team members time for rest and reflection, but not too distant. To complete and report within two weeks, as an initial target, is often reasonable.

Workflow Management

If task tracker functionality is implemented, most such systems can be extended to provide workflow management and prioritisation. Where you have implemented one or more incident management flowcharts, such as those described in Chapter 12, the tracker can be used to pass activities to the next stage, or responsible individual or group.

Note that a significant degree of flexibility will need to be incorporated to permit activities to appropriately assigned within the wide range of actual incidents. In particular, some incidents will be relatively trivial therefore a number of steps may well be skipped for efficiency. Additionally, the incident manager should be able to reassign activities or to move the workflow forward or back within the process. In the notes attached to these decisions, the justification for those should be recorded, as close to the time of taking the decision as possible to able the PIR to present them in context.

Attachments

Working Documents

Unless you are granted a particularly flexible incident management system, there will be a need to draft and manage documents, spread sheets and data bases on normal office IT systems. Where documents are critical, these should be held in team shared areas and links included as part of the incident narrative. It is also important to remember the comment made earlier that any notes should be copied in a format that would resist damage if fast system shutdown is required. If possible, good version control should be maintained so that PIR can review detailed changes in understanding of causes and impacts.

Issued Document Versions

Where the system permits, key issued documents, such as management, customer or regulator briefings should be held on the incident system. Ideally, these should be in some form of protected or semi-protected format, whether this is achieved through removing edit permissions within a DRM environment or by printing the documents to formats such as Adobe PDF.

Note that many such documents will continue to be updated, therefore a copy of each release version should be retained and titled in a manner that the order of the versions is understood both in terms of readers and generators of such documents within the team.

Evidence Packs

Where detailed evidence packs are produced for disciplinary or court action because of the sensitivity and potential content, it will generally be inappropriate to record anything more within the incident record other than the date and time of completion and the distribution list.

Evidential Integrity

Using the incident management system to record information that requires formal establishment or maintenance of chain of custody/ chain of evidence is not recommended, as this will significantly increase the complexity of the system and the storage volume requirements and may result in large quantities of additional data needing to be considered for disclosure.

In common law jurisdictions, material recorded on the incident system is likely to be admissible under the business records exemption to the hearsay rule, however this cannot be used to avoid the need for integrity maintenance for the records of invasive investigations

However, it may be appropriate to additionally record key integrity information within the incident management system, as well as in the investigators contemporarious notes. In a large organisation which has a forensic case management system, links to key records or reports may be also be appropriate to include those in the IMS narrative.

Generating Reports

It may be possible to generate and pre-populate standardized report templates from the details available in the IMS whether through IMS functionality or an additional tool-set. Incident meta data current and previous IM summaries, current and completed tasks may all be useful in generating end of shift, daily or other regulator or ad-how reports. If this is not available, having pre-prepared templates where manual cut and paste can be used will still save time. Please note that it is essential that non-statistical reports are pre-drafted, rather than pre-generated. Particularly if the audience is senior management or otherwise non-technical judicious editing and even "translation" will materially improve the readability and ultimately utility of reports.

Summary Reporting

If you have reporting functionality and are unlucky enough that you deal with multiple incidents, the ability to generate reports for the

IR hierarchy and their executive sponsors is also very useful. Typical reporting may include:

- All incidents initiated during a set period with the current IR summary.
- A list of all open incidents, with or without the current IR summary.

List of all current tasks or activities with the responsible individual and the next review and expected due times. Where incidents are less common this sort of information should be able to be easily manually extracted.

Team Metrics

One of the great problems in information security, given its unfortunate status as the reification of a privative, is the construction and use of reasonable and informative metrics. Incident response is one of the areas where this seems to be more achievable than in others, such as security architecture. When you are starting out on the process of formalizing your incident response strategy and framework, simple measures are readily reportable.

Number of Incidents Open

Time taken to close incidents (obviously more information as some sort of statistical distribution than a simple number) and IR team utilization should all be reasonably easy to report on, even if they cannot be produced automatically within the recording system. As experience of post-incident reviews and subsequent discussion with wider stakeholders grows, you will be able to refine existing metrics and develop new and pertinent ones.

Need to Know

Many investigations will involve or uncover corporately, commercially or personally sensitive information, even if the overall investigation is not being treated as "special handling." With the increasing focus on corporate data leakage and personal privacy, it is essential that the security management system itself does not become a source of issues, or even incidents. You may be lucky enough to have sufficiently granular control of access privileges to restrict access to particularly sensitive information or reports. Alternatively, you may be able to split the relevant area off as a separate "sub-incident" with fewer participants. In either case, this should be noted in the incident narrative.

Where automated reporting is available it is important to ensure that this works on the basis of individual users' access rights, rather than full system access to avoid inadvertent disclosure. It may be considered that some fields within any incident record should be open to all system users. Typical fields would be:

- The incident reference
- Date of opening and closing
- PIR date
- Incident status
- Current incident manager
- Other fields will depend on your organisation and how you record certain details.

If you are operating within a government or other formal information classification environment, you may also need to consider "cleared to know"; however, this is usually managed by ensuring that IR personal have a common and high level of clearance.

Incident Meetings

One of the critical occasions where the incident, priorities and activities are discussed, are your regular incident meeting. There obviously needs to be some record of these within the system. Full minutes are probably inappropriate, both because of the resource required and the potential sensitivity of some of the discussion, particularly where unusual solutions are being proffered and debated.

People are likely to propose things that are decided to be inappropriate or impractical and free discussion should not be hampered by making any and all comments part of a formal, and auditable record. However, in certain jurisdictions or regulatory environments, and for certain types of incident, this 100% recording may be imposed.

A usually more acceptable format is the Record of Actions and Decisions (often referred to as "ROADS") which is reasonably self-explanatory.

Revealing the Case Studies

Amber Inc.

Because Amber Inc. is a multinational organisation ensuring the appropriate information in the course of an incident is not a going to be straightforward. There are going to be legal and regulatory requirements in a number of countries, some of which will be similar or even identical, but others are going to be specific to a jurisdiction.

It is to be hoped that, if there is an incident response team already operating, that the various legal and regulatory requirements have already been identified, even if they have yet to be brought together into a formal process. However, even if you are taking over such a team you would be well advised to go carefully through the recording process and both check it is operationally sound, that it covers all requirements and that you understand it. If any of those aspects are weak, show signs of hasty design, or are difficult for someone coming in to understand, then scheduling a formal review of the process, with any concerns you have or that have been highlighted in any recent post-incident reviews should be a priority. After all, if something goes wrong responsibility will point back to you as the person responsible for the conduct and recording of incidents.

Jade Ltd.

Because the sensitive nature of the data that Jade Ltd. deals with and the high profile nature of their customers, it is clear that the recording of incident response handling information appropriately is essential. It would be a worthwhile exercise to extract all the requirements of notification or other action, in a situation that may affect their data, from your joint contract and check those along with the suggestions made above. Unlike for Amber Inc., there are less likely to be an international dimension with regard to legal requirements. If there are any doubts, then it is worth getting this checked by an appropriately knowledgeable person. This may be a lawyer, but the cost of their time is unlikely to exceed the cost, financial and in terms of damage to reputation, of crossing fingers and hoping you have it right. There may be requirements that are specific to their operations, or a legacy of previous incidents, that is not included in our list above. It is vital that those requirements, along with those from the recommendations above, be considered in devising an information recording process. We have found that the most effective way of devising a workable process for this purpose be informed from a workshop or table top exercise with as many interest parties as possible.

As Jade Ltd. is just a medium sized organisation, spread across a number of sites, incident response may well use staff from a number of different teams, so it is even more important that all those taking part understand the reason behind the recording process and are comfortable with how to use it. As so many of these records rely on contemporaneous notes, it might prove difficult to attempt to construct them retrospectively in the event that someone failed to record adequately.

Having said all of that, the fact that the nature of their business has the protection of highly sensitive information at its heart, should mean that more staff will have an appreciation of the importance of proper handling of all incidents. That is not to say that they won't resist additional bureaucracy in incident handling, but any resistance should be manageable.

19

POST-INCIDENT REVIEW

Let us not look back in anger, nor forward in fear, but around us in awareness.

James Thurber

When experience is not retained, as among savages, infancy is perpetual.

George Santayana
Reason in Common Sense

Information in this chapter:

- Nobody's perfect
- Formal verses informal
- Defined outputs
- But we don't need these?

Introduction

As has been said or implied elsewhere, post-incident review is the most important bit of incident response. Effective post-incident reviews are what separates the merely competent teams from the actually good. It is, however, also the easiest bit to gloss over or conduct in a shallow way, aiming not to draw attention to mistakes. Even people who appreciate its importance can be tempted to focus on ensuring a good review as the relief of being able to categorise an incident as closed or complete is generally stronger than the desire to review the handling of the incident in order that lessons can be learnt.

Conducting a thorough review, especially of a complex incident can be, in the words of the sage*, a "courageous" thing to do.

To conduct an effective review requires a level of honesty which, even without the associated self-reflection, is difficult in many organizations. Often, it is politically difficult (which translates quickly as career suicide) not least because it may require people, even management, to accept fault. Senior management who have some responsibility for the action of an individual or team whose action may have contributed to the incident can find it difficult not follow the cultural norm of punishing people if they are formally identified at fault.

For these and many other reasons, effective PIRs are not carried out nearly as often as they should be, even in organizations with otherwise mature incident management.

Starting

When an incident nears completion, there is a sense of relief that the solution has been arrived at, and it may appear work can get back to normal. However, one key action cannot be dismissed, however strong the desire to do so and that is the post-incident review (PIR). In fact, there are circumstances when it may be necessary to conduct two PIRs, once when the incident is still ongoing and once when complete. Depending on the nature of the incident, there may be extended actions – that is actions that will take longer than the period covered by the actual incident to complete. Examples include those involving disciplinary, legal or technical fixes that may not be possible to complete instantly or even quickly. If an employee is fired for reasons associated with the incident, the legality of that action may be taken to an employment tribunal, which may in turn reveal mistakes in the process of handling the incident, which would need to be considered. Waiting until such extended actions are complete before conducting the PIR would remove many of the benefits, including fresh memories of actions taken and dynamic changes in operations, policies, procedure or other areas that may have contributed to the incident. This would reduce the effectiveness of the PIR, so it is suggested that

---

* Sir Humphrey Appleby, as played by Sir Nigel Hawthorne in the TV series *Yes Prime Minister.*

a provisional PIR be conducted as usual, then a final, closing PIR once those external actions are closed.

Another reason why it might be sensible to take a slightly different approach to a PIR would be if there were a number of similar incidents that took place close together. In this case, it may be reasonable to combine the PIRs to avoid repetition and pool knowledge from all those involved in the various incidents.

Because of the importance of having the fullest possible information relating to the incident, it is unhelpful for the PIR to used as the place for attributing blame to individuals as opposed to it being an honest forum where those involved in the PIR can discuss both the successes of the incident handling as well as about mistakes or errors that may have happened.

Unless the security incident was specifically investigating individual misconduct (whether one person or a group), it is important not to allow the review to become a forum for identifying the sacrificial goat on which to blame the event or its handling. Frankly, even in those cases, the security incident should be gathering evidence and presenting it to a different, non-incident forum, whether a corporate disciplinary hearing, an arbitration tribunal or external regulators or law enforcement.

"Blame hunting" not only inhibits frank discussion for the incident in review, but it can have a signification effect on people's willingness to co-operate with future security incident response incidents.

What Is the Purpose?

The purpose of the PIR is to identify any successes as well as improvements required in either the incident management process or in the wider organizational security posture and procedures. However, things being the way that they are, the general focus is on identifying any fixable negatives.

Although the details of what needs to be considered will vary from incident to incident and between organizations, the following are a useful baseline:

- Were there inappropriate delays in detecting or reporting the incident?

- Did the incident management process appropriately and effectively deal with the incident?
- What was the underlying cause of the incident?
- Using 20/20 hindsight, are there specific things that can be learned for future similar incidents? It is important to realise that this is very different from the process question. A positive answer may very well be that a useful contact should be added to your lists, or there is a need to increased awareness of the relevant laws in a specific jurisdiction.
- Is/was there a material weakness in the organization's security posture or controls? Was this known about and, if so, subject to proper risk treatment & management?
- Estimate the cost of the incident both in terms of loss of business (often very hard), as well as in the cost of investigation time and materials.

Depending on the size of the organization, the seriousness of the incident and the amount of information available, the PIR can be convened formally or as a less formal meeting.

Regardless, of how formal the meeting is, some record should be taken of any decisions made or actions arising.

Who Should Be Involved?

- The PIR should be chaired by an experienced incident manager, but not the manager of the incident itself.
- Any other incident manager or managers who became involved.
- Lead technicians.

When conducting a more formal PIR, you should consider involving the following:

- Internal advisors such as HR, Legal or Customer/Media Relations where there was significant involvement within the incident.
- IT where there was a significant availability component or where significant emergency changes were required to IT state.
- Communications provider/ISP, data-centre and BCP specialists (internal or external) where there was significant involvement.

Notification

There is an important distinction between:

- When an incident actually occurred.
- When it was first detected by the organization.
- When it was first notified to somebody (or invokes some process) that could reasonably deal with the situation.

Here, you should be concentrating on any unreasonable delay between the initial identification of the incident and the official notification. Delays between when the incident occurred and when it was detected would generally fall under the controls improvements section of the PIR.

Incident Management Process and Procedures

There are a number of things to consider here:

- Is this a new category of incident?
- In the course of handling the incident did the team find they had to deal with a legal jurisdiction that they were largely unfamiliar with?
- Did the team receive (or need but not receive) new or updated legal guidance?
- Was the incident management process appropriately followed? Remember – it is guidance for the confused rather than a rigidly prescriptive rail-road. However, some elements such as executive or regulator notification may be mandatory and distinctly time-bound.
- Did this progress of this incident highlight any flaws or omissions in the incident management process? As with the previous question, it is useful to remember that except where it is legally unwise to do so, the incident manager should have a degree of flexibility in interpreting the various procedures. It is important not to bind future incident response by making procedures too specific. However, the manager will be accountable for the way procedures were followed or otherwise.
- Were the processes easily and fully understood? It may be that, they need to be re-written in a simpler style? The original

author may be your expert in that particular area and might have assumed too much knowledge on the part of the actual responder, or they may be using niche jargon.

- Does any of the detailed guidance (system descriptions, business restrictions, contact details) need to be updated?

Communications

Was your communications,within the team and with partners, suppliers and specialist advisors adequate throughout the incident? Did you manage to get hold of people where you expected to find them and within the required (or contracted) timescales?

Were there unexpected issues with any communications equipment, such as unforeseen impacts from the incident itself? For example, if much of your communications relies on passing documents by email, an incident affecting the email system will be problematic.

In one notorious incident over a weekend, Matthew managed to destroy two batteries for his mobile phone. They simply could not keep up with being partially charged while he was using the other battery, and then flattened while that one was on charge.* As Matthew does like to pace when he is thinking, having the phone on charge while he was using it wasn't ideal. Three new batteries and an additional charger were acquired the following week.

Equipment

Were there:

- Shortages of equipment or unavailability of internal or contracted services?
- Problems that delayed access to the required equipment or services?
- Equipment or service failures?

---

* This was, of course, an earlier generation of batteries. With modern lithium cells, he might have ended up with minor burns to his ear. However, with modern lithium batteries, that is not the worst thing that could've happened.

- Equipment not up to date (for example, for patching or version updates)?
- Did one of the partner organizations use, have or mention a piece of equipment that might help in future incidents?*

Root Cause Analysis

Hopefully, there should have been some cause analysis conducted on the incident. If not, this should be a key part of the PIR and should not just consider the proximate cause of the incident but all contributory factors.

As an example, the obvious cause may have been an external hack attempt (motive, at this stage, not being material), but this may only have worked because the server was running a legacy operating system and, for reasons considered or otherwise, was not up to date for patching.

- If the server was not deliberately un-patched,† how is the patching managed?
- Is there an automated system, or are patches implemented manually? Did the organization patching system fail or does it not reach these particular elements?
- Was the server missing just one or a small number of patches or has it remained un-patched for some time?
- Where the cause contain an element of patching you might consider the following:

    - Is it, in fact, on the automated or manual list for patching?
    - If not, why not? Has the server been implemented without going through the normal controls/change management process or has the process failed?

---

* Of course, beware of the besetting flaw of the technically-gifted: "shiny-toy syndrome." Be realistic about the cost-benefit of any new device.
† Legacy application compatibility means this is actually much more common than security architects would desire. There's still plenty of NT4 server running in various places, never mind the millions of lines of Cobol that support business and safety critical services.

- If it is, why has the patch process not worked? Is there, for example, a permissions issue or was there a network fault when the patch was due?*
- Has the system recorded that the patch was implemented whereas, in reality, it either wasn't attempted or it failed?

Similarly, a sensitive data loss may be obviously and trivially due to an employee downloading material on to an unencrypted USB drive which they then lose. Or material may be on the personal cloud of a staff member who has left, become ill or died. This might be a failure to abide by organizational policy or have been necessary at the time.†

Obviously, reasons may vary dependant on incident type, but there may be lessons to be learnt. Was the team under severe pressure to meet deadlines? Were there no secure alternative ways to move the data (and, frankly, are these secure alternatives efficient and easy to use)? Why has the organization not implemented one of the blocking technologies to restrict access for anything bar officially issued, encrypted USB sticks? Actually, does the organization make encrypted USB sticks readily available?

Often, unfortunately, and especially where service restoration has been given priority, there might not be sufficient information to do a proper analysis. In which case, do what can be done and note why the analysis is limited.

Hindsight

If you are managing incidents properly, mistakes will be made.

Incident managers will need, as has been discussed before, to make decisions based on limited and even inadequate evidence. There should not be any part of the process that discourages them from making necessary decisions, even if they turn out to be wrong. And there may have been good and valid reasons for that particular decision at the time it was needed. And of course this should be recorded in your incident management system.

---

* The obvious follow-up question being, in that case, why wasn't the patch re-tried when the network fault was rectified?

† Of course, if both of these are true, that is probably indicative of a wider issue.

- Decisions made incorrectly because of incorrect information need to be explored as to whether there is a redeemable defect, rather than merely an error, in the information gathering process.
- It is necessary to be careful when reviewing decisions made incorrectly because there was a lack of information. The various pressures on the incident manager at the time are difficult to reconstruct and, even if that is managed, to interpret rationally. For example, where information had been sought, but there was a delayed in accessing it, it may have been necessary to make the decision in its absence. This may indicate flaws in the information gathering and communicating process. However, a possible key factor to validate is whether the decision maker was aware that they were making the decision in the absence of specific elements that they would have preferred to have present.
- Where information was available but was not used by the incident manager this may indicate an issue with intra-team communications or a learning point for the individual or team.

Special Handling Cases

Often, for special handling cases, it is worth scheduling two post-incident reviews. The initial review might cover the period from notification up to the delivery of the evidence pack, looking at issues including authorisation, legality and acquiring, filtering and presenting the evidence, as well as the more generic incident management issues covered above for standard incidents.

A subsequent review, following the completion of the disciplinary or legal action, should consider:

- The competence of the evidence pack presented
  - Admissibility.
  - Completeness.
  - Any recommendations regarding competence based on initial analysis of the evidence.*

---

* It is quite legitimate for a investigation to conclude that there is probably insufficient evidence for a safe or successful, disciplinary or legal case, but for the organization to progress it regardless.

- Appropriateness of the relevant investigation procedures.
- Any developments in understanding of the legal circumstances surrounding the particular or similar cases.
- It may also be necessary to look at the interfaces between the disciplinary and investigations processes, although the HR or legal teams should also be reviewing their process and actions in light of the final outcome.

Costs

Incident cost estimates, particularly those that are paraded through the press for example used as evidence of damage in hacking court cases or are featured in industry surveys are not generally reliable, and therefore not useful for evaluating costs likely incurred in an incident. For example, these normally these report a significant over-estimate in the cost of time taken.

The resource and direct expenditure costs for any incident should be reasonably easy to quantify to an acceptable degree of accuracy. Costs to the business in terms of immediate and long-term losses of custom will be far less easy to guess and probably impossible to calculate. However, any estimate produced by the business is worth recording as part of the overall measurement of incident effectiveness, particularly as it may help justify future investment in incident response and management.

Mitigating Future Similar Incidents

We have a mutual, what the merchant navy refer to as a "board of trade acquaintance," i.e. a professional in our field, who insists that the answer to any legal question is "It depends."

Unfortunately, he is right.

Unless you are one of the unfortunates who are deluged with similar security issues, in which case you should rapidly develop processes to deal with your more common problems, one of your major learnings will be "Can we make this less of an issue for the organization next time?"

Unfortunately, in many or even most occasions, the answer is "no." Attacker motivations and techniques are likely to be very different, even if the attack vector is very similar. Conversely, an attacker motivation of stealing money from you doesn't particularly indicate any competence or attack approach. However, in many industry sectors, particularly for criminal attackers, the cash out possibilities are relatively circumscribed therefore, any innovative attack is likely to give you some considerable understanding of the end to end criminal intent.

In some cases, the manager can learn really quite quickly and put in place effective strategies to mitigate attacks at the early stages. This may enable you to drive a particular issue down from "incident" to "issue"* to "scripted problem" and then solution inside a year. This was probably lucky, but it may be possible to prescribe detailed responses to specific attack types, based on your organization's risk and impact models. On the other hand, for example, where reputational threat is paramount, even trivially common attack vectors such as "phishing" may still need a individually-assessed and appropriately-authorized response.

If you feel that you sufficiently understand the totality of the attack its causes and its impacts and that those impacts are not politically sensitive within your organization, you may be able to construct a model for dealing with similar events in a more methodological way. However, as this does this opportunity is not always available this should be seen as a desirable outcome rather than a target.

However, it is always nice to be able to drop something down from the incident manager to the investigating technician so they can earn their allowance.

Always be aware that trivial changes in any of target, technique or motive can render pre-scripted responses ineffective, or especially if the attacker has had multiple attempts, actively harmful.

Although the concept of moving stuff "down-stack" is likely to enthuse you, maintaining flexibility of both thought and response is essential.

If you decide to produce a process or guide as a result of your incident experience this needs to be tested against future incidents before it is brought in to be formal practice.

---

* Matthew has certainly dealt with types of issues that turned from having to be dealt with as a crisis into business-as usual issues over repeated regular incidents – phishing attacks were the most obvious of these.

Revealing the Case Studies

Amber Inc.

Amber Inc. has a number of issues that will affect the way that post-incident reviews can happen. The fact that Amber Inc. is a multinational company means it will need to be able to access knowledge of a range of issues, legal or otherwise, of their base country, as well as others where they have operational concerns. This applies not only in the course of the handling of an incident, but also in reflecting on it in the PIR.

At the time of setting up the IR function, there would already be experience within the organization of dealing with issues across their various regions through the IT team. Accessing this knowledge may hit some of the challenge that is so difficult in a general PIR – that identifying, especially self-identifying, people who were involved in previous events and who learnt from mistakes as well as good practice may be hard. If these people are not part of the new IR function, and especially if their experience was negative, they may be unwilling to taint their current role with mistakes of the past. Of course, there is also the fact that unless careful note was taken, which is less likely until the IR function was devised, then memory decay would affect the reliability of the information gathered. However, as many experiences of dealing with the sort of issues that are likely to affect the new IR team, as can be identified will help with identifying knowledge and skills that should be accessible by the internal team.

Jade Ltd.

Jade Ltd.'s greatest concern is with regard to the very sensitive nature of data that it processes. By definition, any incident that impacts on the integrity or security of any of that information is a serious incident. In simple terms, the cannot be seen to be taking anything less that total care of the sensitive data. It is also important to recognise that there are only around four people and a manager in the internal IT team. This means that IR, while the overall responsibility of Jade Ltd. (especially with the changes brought in by the General Data Protection Regulations, which came into force across Europe in May 2018) is going to rely on external staff for a lot of the work, so the

PIR is going to have to be handled with care and mutual respect. The possibility of blame for shortcomings, mistakes or misunderstandings, bouncing between both IT teams is real. Given this is a situation where all efforts must be placed on the protection of the data, efforts, especially with regard to training and exercises, need to be run in order to develop understanding of IR in co-ordination.

However, when the incident is over and the PIR is being carried out it will be harder to honestly identify strengths and weaknesses of the running of the incident. The external contractor has little incentive to admit errors. Why would they point out mistakes that might lead to a loss of trust in their operations? In normal circumstances, this is not rational. How well PIRs operate in situations like this will depend on how well the teams work together and trust each other. An obvious approach to achieving this would be to involve representatives from the external contractor to table-top exercises and workshop events with the internal team. This way they will get to know and understand each other and built a join understanding of the way IR needs to operate to be effective for Jade Ltd.

Without doubt, having the two teams working together is a potential weak point in the IR process, but it could, if properly handled, provide strength. For example it potentially gives Jade access to more specialists in different area of IT, and even IR, than they would have in their own organization, and this could also provide valuable feedback and improvements in process through the PIR meetings.

20
NETWORK AND SECURITY MONITORING

It wasn't by eliminating the impossible that you got at the truth, however improbably: it was by the much harder process of eliminating the possibilities. You worked away, patiently asking questions and looking hard at things.

Terry Pratchett
Feet of Clay

Information in this chapter:

- Network operations centre
- Security operations centre
- Specific security concerns and tools
- Legal concerns about monitoring

Introduction

There are a wide variety of tools and services that can provide real or near-real time information about your network, both interior and perimeter. Although some of these tools may be part of your armoury, it is more usual that specialist teams operate these. The first task of any incident response manager is to inventory what is, and what could be, made available to you.

In many organizations, long before they get around to having dedicated security operations teams, a centralized "Network Operations," usually just called "The NOC" (pronounced "knock"), is created. This is often primarily, if not solely, focused on systems and network availability.

An organization may have an outsourced security operations centre, looking at a wide range of differing inputs and conducting correlation assessments to determine whether errors or issues show significant indicators of malicious attack or compromise, or are just the sort of random things that go wrong if you look at a large enough number of computers.* Depending on the contract with the SOC, they may merely be assessing technical feeds or form a more integral part of your incident assessment and triage functions. However, it is important to remember that not all incidents would be identified by the SOC. For example, allegations of sexual harassment by email will probably not have any indicators, positive or negative, that would make their way to the SOC data feeds.

In addition, there are other toolsets that can be of considerable use. A network operations team may have access to data such as net flows, which can provide vital information if data exfiltration is a particular concern. Also, there are special monitoring tools that will be covered at the end of the chapter.

Network Operations Centre

From a security perspective, the network operations centre is rarely an ideal partner. Their tool sets tend to be designed for efficiency and low network impact, rather than the accuracy, sometimes to a forensic level, that is generally preferable in order to provide basic security context and status. However, as well as basic system availability, information network operations centre may have access to a large range of useful data. Patch and antivirus status will usually be available and can notify systems that could be vulnerable to a particular suspected attack. System performance and network utilization data can indicate something is going awry on the network particularly if there is a basic record of what "normal behaviour" looks like. It is important to appreciate that network usage is likely to look very different at 9 P.M. on a Sunday night, as opposed to 12 hours later, even if Monday is a holiday!

---

* If you have an internal SOC, your security posture is probably sufficiently robust that this book is not aimed at you.

Of particular importance to an organization is its ability to have networks team operate robust logging and monitoring, although this needs to be balanced against its likely business impact. While it may be identified as desirable to be able to undertake real time network capture, this is generally not permanently enabled on any network segment, and if it is, those are unlikely to be segments of particular interest in an IR context.

An IR manager might argue that effort is ongoing to ensure that they work with the relevant specialists and their managers in order to understand their baseline capabilities and the extras that are available. This is especially important in a reactive, rather than a proactive context. It is also important to be aware of any technical or operational limitations those extra capabilities might be expected to introduce. It may be necessary to duplicate capability, for example by having dedicated portable security capture devices so as to limit impact on the usual NOC services. It is worth remembering that a sophisticated attacker may attempt to cover their traces by initiating a large and obvious attack at the same time as a more focused attack with a high-impact payload.

Especially where incident management operations don't have a dedicated or convertible room, it can be useful to have the ability to display the NOC dashboard.

Where any incident has a gross impact on any systems within the NOC scope, a supervisory member of the NOC shift should be included in technically-focused incident meetings.

The Security Operations Centre (SOC)

The SOC will have a range of security tool sets and expertise that allow them to provide a more focused analysis than their network counterparts. However, as the SOC is unlikely to be in control of active devices on your network, it is important to be aware that pre-configured data streams that are being fed to them are likely to fundamentally limit their capability. It would be very unusual for a SOC not to have access to logs from security specific devices such as firewalls and IDS/IPS, however, they may not have access to all network devices that provide some degree of security enforcing function or to devices at a sufficiently low level to answer detailed questions about; for example, whether a change in an executable file was due to an authorized process or evidence of some sort of attack.

Where a company is fortunate enough to have very few security incidents, the learning curves of the SOC team and the IR teams will be steeper for all involved, as the SOC becomes familiar with how business treats security incidents, as well as how the manager in charge of IR wants incidents involving the SOC are going to be handled.

The primary purpose of a SOC is to aggregate and correlate a wide range of disparate security relevant feeds and to identify those security events which, while not necessarily yet an incident, are indicative of needing more detailed investigation. Some SOCs may be capable of conducting that next investigation stage, but, particularly with large out-sources, they have the advantage of a view across a much wider ecosystem than any individual one of their customers. Although some attacks will be tailored to specific vulnerabilities in your organization, it should be expected that a numerically much larger proportion of attacks are significantly more generic, meaning the targets are any available victim, possibly within a specific industry or other sector, rather than attacking a specific organization. Not only does this wider view enable the SOC to raise an alert as the trail of attackers moving from target to target becomes clearer, but if the attack isn't just blasted across the network, the SOC may have also been able to pre-prepare appropriate mitigating counter-measures before your organization is affected, or even attacked.

As with the NOC, it is a matter of working with the SOC, to understand their capabilities and limitations and how they can best fit into the overall incident team structure. Unfortunately, unlike the NOC, the SOC is likely to have much less flexibility to increase the depth of monitoring in periods of tension. However, there may be additional sensors and tool kits that the SOC can bring in that would help with that so it is worth understanding what capabilities these bring and exploring both the contractual and configuration change requirements to enable these if they are required.

Specific Security Concerns and Tools

As well as the standard security tools available with firewalls IDS IPs and router ACLs, there are a number of more specialist tools that may provide useful information for assessment and triage. SEIM (Security Event and Incident Management) tools will not be covered here as they are the primary equipment for a SOC.

Indicators of Compromise

One of the data sets that are important with looking for from any monitoring capability are indicators of system compromise, usually just referred to as "IoCs." These are specific events on a device that are characteristic of generic attack success (for example, creation of new privileged accounts) or more specific indicators of the successful function of one or more attack tools; for example, the creation of a new executable file or the modification of an existing system or application executable.

Whereas many security tools look for the network or file signatures of attacks, which can be trivially masked by even basic encryption or other techniques such as polymorphism, IoCs look for the impacts of the operation of an attack tool. While the main compromise impacts are obvious thing to look for, as they are the desired effects of the tools designer, they can be deliberately changed in ways that mask detection. Many IoC tools also look for side effects of attacks. These may be artifacts of the attacker's development environment or due to programming errors or shortcuts, and therefore they may either be more difficult to change or simply not recognised by the attacker.

As well as being able to extract IoCs from any existing monitoring toolset, there are specialist tools available designed purely to detect compromise usually from network traffic monitoring. The main difficulty with these is ensuring that they are on a suitable network segment, within their capacity to conduct 100% traffic monitoring, and yet with a wide enough view of your network entry and exit traffic to provide a comprehensive service. Obviously, you also need to ensure that they are monitoring clear-text traffic.

Data Exfiltration

In many cases, after their obvious concern about availability, the primary concern of the business will be whether any data has been lost. The mere compromise of a system even one that contains or potentially has access to sensitive data, while worrying does not imply that any sensitive data has actually been viewed or copied (in so far as there is any substantive difference between those terms in the digital context) by the attacker. Being able to provide appropriate evidence to inform the analysis of this question is critical. This requires knowledge of where your data is flowing, and ideally, to be able to drill down into this aggregate data to focus on those systems either which might appear to be compromised or those which hold your most sensitive data. If the brochureware web server is suddenly, and unexpectedly, communicating with the CRM or financial systems this is ought to be a significant concern. On the other hand, your transactional webserver may be supporting several hundred of your customers and totally reasonably communicating with your accounting and stock management systems. If this load suddenly leaps to several thousand ongoing sessions and these sessions are either coming from a small range of IP addresses or have "bot-net" indicators, then this again is of material concern.

Wider awareness of network connectivity and rates of data exchange should also be a matter of concern. Compromise of your office administration estate, which often has access to the organization's most critical business information as well as personal information on both staff and customers, may lead to data exfiltration, often by well explored but obscured routes. The IR manager may get some benefit from data loss prevention tool sets if installed, so it is important that getting access to the reporting tools available from those is explored.

Here, as with so many other aspects of incident detection, it helps significantly if there is a clear understanding of normal operation looks like. There may be a large customer in, say, Indonesia, who places a single huge, set of orders every quarter. Although that is likely to show up as an attempt of interest in reasonably configured monitoring environment, being aware of this event in advance will help it to be dealt with appropriately and in an efficient, business-like manner. Of course, the purchasing manager at the customer may have use been sacked and may be trying to sneak a fraudulent order in by mimicking his usual behaviour and hoping you don't notice the minor differences. Nobody said this was going to be easy.

Distributed Denial of Service (DDoS)

Much effective DDoS protection will take place outside of scope of monitoring for most organizations, their ISP, or at their higher tiers. However, it is likely there will be some detection capability at your perimeter, network and security devices or with specific DDoS devices or components. As has been previously mentioned, knowledge of what is normal is vital. Traffic patterns on your network will vary considerably and, as with other security tools configuring so that false positive alarms are minimized, is essential. That was a very specific use of language; you can minimize false positive reports with the potential consequent rise in false negatives, this being an underlying function of adjusting the specificity of the reporting test case. Alternatively, more intensive analysis could be used, leaving the reporting at a relatively low specificity, but then employing additional tests and conditions before raising any alarm.

It is especially important to be aware of DDoS against services that the business relies on. The classic cases of this are attacks against the DNS system. You may be in control, whether directly or by contract, of your authoritative DNS provision and therefore have access to metrics which can help you determine whether or not that service is under DDoS attack. However, a similar and common vector for attack is via blocking or compromising the services by which your customers access (resolve) your DNS. You are unlikely to have any relationship with their suppliers and almost certainly no view of the services they use. With previous clients where this was a significant problem, having either the customer services or security teams having access to a small range of (locally) common ISP connections has been useful in indicating differences between the 'customer' experience from your (hopefully secure) network and normal ISP* access.

There are many different sorts of DDoS attacks. However, the underlying principle is that all resources are fundamentally limited and depend on if an attacker can consume a significant proportion of any one of the victim's vital resources either using techniques where the resource cost to them and their target are significantly unbalanced or using resources that they simply don't care about. In such a case, they

---

* It should be noted that the now common household use of first tier DNS provision - such as Google's Public DNS or Cisco's OpenDNS - is a significant mitigation for this problem but, unfortunately, one outside of your control.

will be able to block some or all of your legitimate users. Assuming the appropriate resources are being monitored, the network operations centre should be able to give warning of rising consumption and of when this hits whatever level is deemed to be critical. Equally, customer service channels, if not affected by the attack, will let you know as soon as customer issues reach the appropriate threshold.

It is difficult to give generic advice on dealing with DDoS attacks, as it very much depends on the exact method being used. Server side compute resource consumption, by repeated TLS session initiation, is very different to gigabytes of apparently legitimate requests being aimed at your DNS servers. Your ISP and SOC are probably the best places to go to for advice, as they are both likely to have seen may more of these than you and the former may be able to throttle or otherwise limit the traffic reaching your affected systems.

Legal Concerns about Monitoring

Depending on your jurisdiction, there may be significant legal restrictions or concerns about the level and type of monitoring you undertake. There may also be a distinction between monitoring that is permanently in place, and any increased level of monitoring that can be deployed during or under suspicion of an attack or other security incident. Even very basic and uncontroversial monitoring, such as anti-virus, will intercept and process emails and files containing sensitive and personal data.

More invasive monitoring may carry a high risk of exposing sensitive material to the monitoring teams and retain it within monitoring systems. "Data protection by design" is essential when designing and implementing monitoring solutions, whether permanent or installable and in many jurisdictions transparency about your monitoring capabilities and the uses of monitoring data is required. Given the fraught nature of privacy concerns and the widely different legal treatment of a business's authority within its own network, it is essential that you co-ordinate with Human Resources and/or legal advisors to ensure you stay within local acceptability.

Where you have systems you feel would benefit from extensive monitoring, this may be another argument in favour of segmenting them away from systems processing more general data.

Revealing the Case Studies

Amber Inc.

Because of the size of Amber Inc. and also because of the external pressure they are under to be able to demonstrate ISO 27001 compliance, it is expected they already have a NOC team. However, they would look to an external provider to operate a SOC.

It is important that Amber Inc. are able to demonstrate an understanding of the data generated by their normal operations, as well as that which might indicate or warn of the building of an attack. There also needs to be a clear process that is triggered by any suspicious event, and a log of what actions are taken, and what their effect is.

Because there is a strong IT team formulating a NOC may be a matter of bringing together functions and system monitoring that are already in operation. It could also be used to record the trigger points for the involvement of seconded staff, which is a significant issue with Amber Inc., not least because of the impact on normal operations of having staff being brought in to assist with handling an incident. In the medium or even long term, this might be helpful to the IR manager if they are trying to get budget for a specialist to be permanently embedded within the IR team.

However, they are going to need to outsource the SOC function as they don't have the full range of skills and time to be able to run a SOC. Also, an external provider would have a greater range of understanding of incident profiles, as they provide analysis to a number of different organizations. A benefit might then be the more ready confirmation of an attack or the identification of an unusual data flow as not suspicious, than one might expect with an internal SOC for an organization for the size of Amber Inc. It is this analysis that is critical with many organizations, and certainly with one with a range of inputs, including those via a customer order capability.

Amber Inc.'s situation is more complicated because of the customer interaction aspect and the increased potential for social engineering attacks or attacks which utilise that within a more complex attack. The training of those who would receive customer reporting is vital in order that they are aware both of what the triggers for alerting are and how to raise that alert. The design of that alert process so that it varies as little as possible, depending on the time of day or night that it is raised is preferable. In the same way, the system for contacting emergency services is nationally identical regardless of where the incident takes place. Indeed, the emergency call system on modern smartphones provides the capability to use it in the same way wherever the caller is. Decisions that come from where the accident has happened are taken at a stage removed from the caller. It is the same with successful incident alerting. The reporter, in this case the person taking a call, chat interface or reading customer email needs only to know that this needs to be reported. Decisions regarding who would deal with the problem and how are best removed from the reporter.

Amber Inc. has both the external requirement to be analysing and handling incidents in a clear, consistent manner. Indeed, it is in bringing together the information from the internal NOC and developing that through the more sophisticated SOC that they will able to refine their processes and evidence their responses for their own development as well as the assurance required by their customers.

Jade Ltd.

While Jade Ltd. is a smaller organization the nature of their work, which includes data analysis, it is most likely that they have staff within the organization that would be able to come together to run both a NOC and a SOC internally. As they have fewer customers, and their communication is more predictable, being able to look at the data traffic and understand what might be indicative of an attack is more straightforward.

However, there is an element that should be considered in the consideration of internal verses external NOC and SOC provision. That is the willingness and capability to provide the level of 24/7 analysis and reporting that effective IR requires. Indeed, as the architecture of the intercommunications between Jade Ltd. and customers such as health providers in the UK is designed to be both robust and carefully monitored by the customer as well, it might be expected that the potential for an incident to be identified within Jade Ltd.'s processes first is small. There certainly needs to be the requirement to react to an incident report very quickly, but is not expected that these would be to be first identified outside normal working frequent enough to justify having a specific 24/7 provision staffed internally.

However, Jade Ltd. would be in a position to work more proactively with any external NOC or SOC providers than Amber Inc. would be. This would present a potential challenge itself, especially when the two parties come to different conclusions, but experience both with actual incidents or with table top exercises, can significantly improve this and enable the total capability to be at least equal to if not exceeding that which either side could provide alone.

The complexity of Jade Ltd.'s use, and relationship with external provision of NOC and SOC is something that will need to be carefully designed and monitored in order to provide the most effective response. This is, of course, especially important to Jade Ltd. given the sensitivity of much of the data they process.

21

SPECIAL HANDLING INVESTIGATIONS

Every normal man must be tempted, at times, to spit on his hands, hoist the black flag, and begin slitting throats.

H. L. Mencken

Information in this chapter:

- What is "special handling"?
- "Need to know" versus "Want to know"
- Differences in handling
- Special HR and legal issues

Introduction

Although the vast majority of investigations can be dealt with under the normal incident response process, there are a range of issues that are sufficiently sensitive that they require to be managed in a much more closed environment and will normally be under more significant pressure and scrutiny from executive management.

Examples of such incidents which will, for most organisations, fall into this category include:

- Leaks of corporate sensitive information to the media.
- Allegations of racial, sexual or other harassment or abuse.
- Corporate gross misconduct offences.
- Possession of illegal material.*
- Resignations of executive management to go to competing organisations.†

---

* This will vary according to the jurisdiction, but will certainly include paedophile imagery.
† Which are usually accompanied by allegations or, at least, significant concerns that they are taking sensitive corporate data with them.

However, depending on the organisational culture, it is often also reasonable to handle all internal investigations in this manner, particularly as taking extra care is generally better than taking insufficient care. It is important to note that some investigations are particularly sensitive and will need to be kept closed, even from other members of the IR team.

While we can't determine exactly what might fall into this category in your organisation, this range of issues indicate some of those where the manager or executive management might wish to restrict details to the smallest possible audience.

It is important to remember that even outside these, victims, witnesses and suspects are likely to all have varying degrees of privacy rights depending on your jurisdiction, so incident details should always be kept under appropriate access control.

It is also worth noting that one of the reasons we involve the wider team in many incidents is to broaden the pool of knowledge and experience from which we can source ideas for overcoming investigations and recovery details.

What Is "Special Handling"?

For those used to government classifications systems, "special handling" can be thought of as a descriptor, a term that can be attached to any event or issue that modifies who has access and how that information is shared and otherwise handled. Here, also it reflects a probably materially different core incident cycle, whereby recovery actions, if they exist at all, are subordinate to the investigation which is contrary to the usual business position and are also much more likely to be non-technical in nature. From the list above, you can see that situations where severe corporate or personal embarrassment, the involvement of the organisational disciplinary system and criminal civil or regulatory legal action may occur, all factor into the decision for any specific event.

Interestingly, although access may be restricted within the team, there often will be situations where it is necessary to share special handling information with a wider variety of internal and external advisors, and it is therefore necessary to have identified secure and reliable ways this can be done in advance.

It is also possible, especially in a smaller organisation, that where the suspect and/or victims are internal staff, there is significant potential for conflict of interest. Matthew and his deputy once found themselves sharing a table at a corporate event with four members of a services team that they were investigating for fraud. Obviously, such situations need to be carefully managed and HR or legal advice should be sought where there is any doubt.

Mileage will vary, but we have found best practice is to endeavour to retain the same incident manager throughout the investigation and allow rotation of the lead and other technicians as required. However, this type of investigation often proceeds more slowly than more IT-orientated issues and, therefore, less out-of-hours working is expected, except in the very early information gathering stages. That means that this can be fit into normal business working patterns.

Depending on the precise nature of the issues in question, you are likely to also have to take more account of your jurisdiction's rules of evidence; therefore, authorities for collection, transmission and storage may need more formal scrutiny than in other issues.

In the case where the incident is triggered by a complaint or tip-off against an individual or group, it is generally impossible to tell at the start of any investigation whether the allegations are justified. Even where they seem possibly sound, there are significant degrees of fault that can be attached to any identifiable individual. It is rarely possible to walk back from an investigation that has been conducted in a technically pragmatic manner to one where the results are competent for admissibility to a court. Care and thoroughness must be exercised. Even if you are convinced that the furthest the matter might go is internal disciplinary, many jurisdictions allow and even encourage sacked members of staff to approach the civil legal system for compensation or in some cases to get their job back, and so the veracity of any investigation needs to be clear.

Where the organisation operates in more than one country, HR and legal advisors for those jurisdictions need to be involved in ensuring IR processes and procedures are sound. Multinational organisations can find to their cost that legal processes can vary dramatically even between neighbouring and otherwise similar jurisdictions. Wendy once found, to her advantage, significant differences between Scottish and English rules for disclosure in the event of a dispute.

"Need to Know" versus "Want to Know"

Throughout his investigations career, Matthew has found that although curiosity might have killed the cat it seems to be the life-blood of the corporate world. Whether it is managers being inappropriately prurient with regard to their staff's behaviour, even when it relates to non-work activities, security consultants interested in why controls improvements have been suggested following an incident or simple interest as to why a member of staff has been suspended or is otherwise absent. While many people may believe they have a justifiable interest in the restricted details of handling investigations, this is one case where it is appropriate that the incident response are the team that says "no." When you are asked for disclosure of special handling material you need to ask yourself three questions:

- Does the person have a legal right to the information without any disclosure exemptions that might apply because the investigation is still in progress?
- Is there an overriding business interest in the release of the information, and if so, what is the smallest fraction that will satisfy this requirement?
- Who is the appropriate authority to take that decision regarding release?

It is essential to learn if there are formally agreed conditions under which it is permitted for investigators to breach the privacy of staff. This should include tight controls about the release of any private or otherwise sensitive information following an investigation. It is also important that general and management reporting on investigations should be restricted to basic statistics rather than including some of the detail that is more appropriate with standard incidents. You may find it necessary to keep records off your usual IR system if there is any question that those access controls are weaker than ideal.

Differences in Handling

Compared to normal investigations of similar priority, special handling investigations are often more driven by reporting to stakeholders. This means that significant changes in both investigations activity and often in core focus will be common. It is rare that an investigation of any size does not uncover significant other matters that appear worthy of investigation, and some of these may be a considerably higher priority than the original incident or investigation.

Careful control of resources and expectancy management with people who may otherwise have little contact with the IR team is vital. If any investigation seems to have a particularly wide variety of incidents, it is often helpful to formally split these out into separate investigations, particularly given usually conflicting disclosure limitations. You will need to be taking advice from a wide range of organisations including HR, fraud investigators, internal or external legal advisors and relevant management. You may also find yourself involved with law enforcement and specialist technical support such as digital forensics. Whereas in more normal investigations there is a very overt trade-off between the propriety of investigatory integrity and the speedy delivery of business focused results, special handling investigations are often significantly more constrained but are usually subject to lesser if still material time pressures. In fact, some common investigations practices such as restoring from historic email back-up or forensic imaging can take considerable amounts of time in themselves.

If an IR manager finds themself responsible for many of these, it is well worth cultivating a solid working relationship with the relevant bits of HR and getting to understand their business process timelines. It is also useful to establish a sequence of standardised reports with notional expected delivery times, following the initial report or, where relevant, the authorisation and commencement of a particular investigations activity.

Special HR and Legal Issues

Dealing with Illegal Material

First, get legal advice.

As the heading suggests, possession of this sort of material is either severely restricted or even illegal. There may be exceptions for corporate investigators but these are often limited and may require specific actions or authorisation. Also, the range of material included in this category is highly dependent on your jurisdiction.

Material such as extreme pornography or material in support of a banned organisation is generally restricted. Other jurisdictions have considerable quirks with regard to the rules for possession or handling. This is a matter one should take with particular care when investigating across borders. Investigators should remain aware of potential issues and where an investigation may have to be paused to determine the appropriate next steps. It is in this sort of situation that the advice we gave earlier, that of cultivating a working relationship with your local law enforcement computer crimes unit, can make a positive difference. This is because the managers hopefully already understand their priorities and limitations, and so they can come to regard the team as a trusted partner in investigations involving your organization, as opposed to one of the suspects.

Assuming that it is appropriate for you to deal with such material, you need to be aware of the practicalities involved. Obviously, an open office environment is rarely suitable for this sort of work. As in so many of these cases, some form of segregated investigations laboratory is required and it is worth either having such a room within your building or have priority, unquestioned use of such a room in the event of need. It is essential that access to this room can be strictly controlled and locked, and, for example, cleaning staff* should be escorted in, and supervised, rather than having default access.

An IR manager needs to be aware that exposure to some of this material can be upsetting or even distressing, and appropriate support should be available to your staff who find themselves unfortunately affected, as already discussed in Chapter 13.

You may also need to keep a separate store of IT for these types of investigations. It is essential that there is the capability to, where appropriate, wipe and rebuild computers, devices and other digital storage-ware between or even during a specific investigation, and that this action is formally recorded. Again, it is worth seeing how colleagues in law enforcement do this, as it may indicate a baseline for process. However, it is important to recognise that they may have special legal privileges and restrictions, which might not wholly apply to those

---

* Also consider out-of-hours security patrols. You may need to consider, especially where compromising material cannot be secured, limiting their access to the investigations room.

outside the legal sector. As above, good legal advice is essential. Also, formal processes and extreme care in handling needs to be undertaken for the output of any material from such investigations.

Conflict of Interest

Unfortunately, it may be the case that a full or associate member of the IR team is the subject of or closely involved in an investigation. In this case, they obviously must play no part in that investigation and, if at all practical, should be removed from all incident activity while that investigation progresses. As a minimum, you should ensure that any privileged access to investigations material and tools is removed. It is also important to record the recognition of that issue and the action taken. The appearance of fairness here is, to a large degree, more important in maintaining the reputation of the IR team than is actually being scrupulously "fair" in any rational sense. If the team is appropriately resourced, a "no-fault" suspension from work or an other absence from the office, such as a training course may be the best way to cope with the issue. With associates it is often similar, as they MAY be able to be left to their "business as usual" activities and simply not involved in IR work. Obviously, where the allegation or issue is sufficiently serious (gross misconduct), your HR processes may require suspension regardless of your pragmatic intent. In any case, ensure formal handovers of any IR activities the person suspected are currently leading are conducted before they are no longer available. When setting up such processes, just remember that they may need to be applied to you.

Revealing the Case Studies

Amber Inc.

Much of the problems Amber Inc. might face in a situation where "special handling" is required are covered above. However, it is worth highlighting a few points.

It is essential that at the earliest stages of setting up any incident response process, advice should be sought in all jurisdictions where business is normally carried out. Some of this may be surprising to someone who is not operating in the region; for example, most outsiders to the UK (and some who live in the UK, come to that) may not be aware of the differences between English and Scots law, both criminal and civil. Baring that in mind, it is best to assume there are significant differences until local authoritative advice specifies where these may be significant, and this advice should be sought at the earliest possible opportunity. The point where an incident that might require "special handling" emerges is generally a bit late as mistakes can easily be made before guidance is in place.

"Special handling" processes should also be consistent with regional and organizational culture. Also, information regarding what such handling is for and how it works should be made available to staff in the normal handbook. Indeed, if a member of staff was under suspicion and, as a result, not allowed access to the organizational network, a copy of the handbook which includes explanation of the process they are involved in should be made available to them.

"Special handling" processes are as much about protecting the innocent as providing evidence against the guilty. Where an organization has its corporate HQ in a different country to the office where the investigation is taking place needs to be able to demonstrate fairness and impartiality in the context of local laws and regulations.

Jade Ltd.

The major issue for Jade Ltd. is likely to be the size of the organisation. We have discussed elsewhere the fact that their size would mean that they need to have more associate members of the IR team, both internal and external. Given that requirement, it may be more difficult to restrict the spreading of details of the incident. It may not be information as such that "leaks," but possibly that an external associate is being used instead of an internal one. Nature and the organizational grapevine generally abhors a vacuum that comes from an absence of information about something of interest. Information, which may be more guess than substance, will rush in to fill the absence and may harm working relationships and reputations.

It is difficult to resist what some see as a natural human behaviour of gossiping, but these suggestions might restrict damage.

- Ensure that all staff understand that the organization takes the need for the protection of all sides of a special Investigation very seriously. This means that all staff should be given a basic understanding of what that process is and why it is used. The key element is to emphasise that being under investigation is not the same as being guilty or at fault.
- Ensure that details of the outline of a special handling process is available to all staff and, as in the example for Amber Inc., that there is a copy for staff who have their access to the internal network suspended.
- All managers should be made aware of their responsibility to discourage their staff from joining in or encouraging speculation about an investigation in the event of an internal special handling case.
- In the event that a member of staff who was the subject of or closely associated with a special handling case be found to have acted appropriately, care is taken to ensure a smooth return to work. Where possible their manager should take care to give overt reassurance of trust of the staff member both personally and within the team.

Where the member of staff was found to have been in a position to have some form of penalty up to and including dismissal, this should be dealt with in such a way that their team is able to return to normal working as soon as possible. In such a small organization, the impact of disruption to even one team or group can often ripple out and cause bad feeling or a drop in work standard in others. However, given that people are dismissed for other reasons besides those investigated in a "special handling" investigation, it is expected that this should not significantly challenge a well-run organization.

22

CRISIS MANAGEMENT AND
DISASTER RECOVERY

And this mess is so big
And so deep and so tall,
We cannot pick it up.
There is no way at all!

Dr. Seuss
The Cat in the Hat

Information in this chapter:

- Types of crisis
- The role of the IR manager in a crisis
- The team
- Disaster recovery

Introduction

As has been said in Chapter 5, the difference between an incident and a crisis is a matter only of degree and when applied in a business environment, who needs to be involved. However, some regard it as a more subjective matter; "One man's crisis is another man's challenge." This may resonate well with positive thinking gurus, but it is an unhelpful way of looking at any ongoing business critical situation because it can mean that that senior-level involvement is not incorporated early enough. This can result in the situation becoming more of a crisis for longer than it needs to be.

Sometimes security IR may find itself part of a larger IR situation. The two key times this will happen are in terms of a disaster recovery situation where there has been a failure at scale of part of the business or its supporting services, or in crisis management where an incident of any cause is having such an impact to the business that it is being run by as senior executive team.

In either case, there will be differences depending on the extent to which IS is part of the cause of the problem or you are merely supporting an incident with a very different cause. For example, a disaster recovery situation resulting from a ransom-ware outbreak will involve you in a very different situation than would be caused by denial of access to premises as a result of a chemical pollution problem.

However, there can be many similarities: the requirement for confident contact with senior members of the organization who may have little or no understanding of the art of the possible and the potentially extensive contact with external bodies such as the media or regulators which will require additional skills and place different working priorities on the IR team as a whole.

There Are a Number of Types or Stages of Crisis

Fundamental Crisis: From the first moment, it is clear that this is a situation of sufficient seriousness that senior management need to be kept informed. In pure business continuity terms, the crisis that resulted from the physical attack on the Twin Towers, leaving aside the human effects or the effects due to the political motivations for the attack, was a fundamental crisis from the moment the first plane hit the first tower. Further, knock on effects from the incident were revealed, but the situation was already a crisis.

Revealed Crisis: This is where the full extent of the problem is not apparent until the incident is being investigated. The nature of the incident does not change, but the full extent of the situation is not clear on first analysis. Following the email trails in an investigation into a mainframe outage, of itself a very significant incident, uncovered a range of serious misconduct ("gross misconduct" in UK employment law terms) amongst hundreds of staff members, including several issues that required to be reported to law enforcement.

Developing Crisis: Subtly different from the revealed crisis, this is where the impact of the issues under investigation increase during the investigation. A phishing attack may be detected after initially targeting a small group of users, but the attackers may release subsequent attack blocks affecting a much larger population. Equally, an initial malware attack might contain a programming error rendering it merely irritating rather than effective and this may be corrected in a second release.

Imposed Crisis: This is an incident that would not, in other circumstances, be a crisis. However, because of other factors such as the public profile of those involved, whether people or organizations affected, the situation needs to be handled with reference to the organization's executive. A phishing attack which overtly targeted high-profile public figures may need to be treated differently at the customer and media management level, even if the underlying technical investigation and corrective actions are identical to those involving the general public.

The Role of Incident Management in a Crisis

Whatever the cause of a crisis, the most valuable asset in successful handling is information. Without information even being able to describe the shape or seriousness of the crisis can be difficult. Until these parameters begin to be defined, gaining control is impossible. Two of the key roles on incident response are to help to gather information about the incident and work to re-establish control of events.

Crisis Management

Where the impact of any incident to the business is such that it poses a significant risk to ongoing business activities or even an existential threat to the organization, good corporate governance requires the executive to play an active part in the management of the problem. As an example, the very large fines introduced with the General Data Protection Regulation, up to 4% of worldwide turnover, are likely to cause material issues for even the most well-funded business. Which, one suspects, was the intention. Equally, allegation or suspicions of gross misconduct against members of the executive themselves or key personnel, while less financially awe-inspiring, may still threaten market confidence or critical business areas or programs. There should not be much surprise if sudden changes in the business focus or direction that you were given emerge. As well as the IR reports, the executive will be receiving guidance from other specialist areas such as legal, regulatory and media relations and that advice may make certain aspects suddenly urgent or even significantly more important than the IR team might have been working under.

Expectancy Management

It has already been mentioned this with regard to reporting upwards and sideways in less serious incidents, but it in a crisis situation it is vital. It is reasonably likely that the executive do not have a glowing opinion of the business competence of IT to which the IR function may be associated, and their understanding of the limits of IR technological capabilities (particularly if funding for that shiny new monitoring or investigations equipment was not forthcoming) will be poor and their tolerance for technical jargon negligible.

Especially where there is a mistrust of IT, let alone IR, it is essential that they have a common and consistent reporting channel which should be the IR manager, in which case that role alone is bound to be a distraction from the active management of the incident. A preferred solution, which is one Matthew has used and recommended in a range of different situations, is that the executive have the IR manager's immediate boss as their contact person. If that is not possible, depending on the size of the organization, it may be possible to bring in a second incident manager or, failing that, rely on an experienced lead technician to take most of the active management burden from you.

Consistency and Simplicity

In order to facilitate this, it is helpful to have a standard reporting template, which should be the same as or very similar to the one you use for slightly less serious incidents.

It should be clear and simple, and lay out the current state of the issue, any actions or decisions you require from them, and provide, in so far as possible, the necessary information for those decisions to be taken. It is essential that reports are provided at the time they are expected, even if this means that they are less complete than ideal. Even if there is a major change in the incident behaviour, it is essential to get a holding report off. The timings that the executives have committed to with regard to their obligations to inform other key stake holders may not have been made clear and an absence of information when the executive need it may hamper the quality of the information they have to pass on.

Media

Nobody should attempt to deal with the media unless they have been properly trained to do so. Ideally, the IR function should not deal with them directly at all; it is best left to corporate communications or media relations specialists, whether internal or external. It is a very good idea to have a set of template forms pre-prepared, discussed and practiced with media relations. These can then easily be populated with the necessary information for the particular event. The most critical thing is never to put any media spokesperson in the position of saying something that is either untrue or that could be, even if true, robustly challenged as misleading or evasive. In particular, underestimating the scale or impact of an issue is unwise. It is worth remembering that particularly with the expansion of locally focused media, modern publishing has meant that an issue can appear much more critical through the lens of different media organizations, especially with their own priorities and prejudices, than it seems to you from the corporate perspective.

The Team

While the team are concentrating on their analysis and reporting, it is important to remember that the communications channel down to those working on the incident, especially where this involved the communication of any changes in priorities or required activities, must be effectively maintained. In both exercises and live incidents, we have seen situations where to an observer it appeared that were two totally different incidents underway, one being competently managed by the blue team and the other well under the control of the white team. Indeed, on the worst occasions, neither bearing much relation to what a third team, the red team, were actually doing. Depending on your background, the requirement to be the hub of a many faceted communications network may be something that you are entirely happy with or something that you need to develop through training and exercise.

Part of the role of the IR manager is to protect the team and its morale from any sudden changes in direction. Obviously, it is not always possible to insulate them from these changes, but if requirements are properly explained and the value of the work the team had been doing up until that point is not undermined, this should minimise the impact on morale. This can mean the manager being in the position of taking a degree of flack from both sides, but that is just one of the perks of the job.

Obviously, if there are significant additional demands from investigation or analysis activities it may be necessary, if practical, to call in additional resource so that the core work, whatever the incident is, can be maintained. Depending on the resources available to you, this may not be immediately available, so careful planning and a degree of honest and considered anticipation will be helpful.

Disaster Recovery

An organization should have a disaster recovery management framework or plan, probably integrated with the lower level business continuity management framework. Those in charge of the IR function need to study this, talk to the responsible practitioners and ensure that the higher levels of your security incident management mesh seamlessly with the disaster recovery plan. Remember that the team can be involved because of security causes or impact of security actions or simply because it is perceived as responsible adults who can valuably assist at a time when is "all hands to the pump." It is also essential the teams' contact details are kept up to date in the business continuity call-out lists.

Revealing the Case Studies

Amber Inc.

Amber Inc., as the larger company of the two here, has the greater opportunity for executives who would normally not be involved in standard IR scenarios, needing to be kept aware of crisis situations.

Also, there may be incidents which fundamentally relate to the physical, non-technical parts of the business, but which impacts areas that are covered by the remit of the IR team. For example, where a catastrophic weather event affects the supply of basic utilities, such as electricity, this may seem to be an access issue for staff, but it can also affect the provision of IT services. Where the organization is larger, it may be that those working in disaster recovery and incident response don't regularly meet. This may not because they don't want to; it may be because they are based on different sites and, in this case, possibly even in different countries. However, there will almost certainly be DR situations which need to have IR input so Amber Inc.'s DL and IR responsible managers should attempt to agree on the approach to situations where IR may be able to contribute positively to the solution.

While co-ordination may sound like such a sensible approach, it would not be contested, there is, in larger organizations like Amber Inc., an additional problem. There is a greater probability of competing egos between IR and DR. Why should one of the team change process in order to suit the process of the other? Especially where both perceive their team as successful, taking a step away from the successful approach could be to reduce the positive career impact for the senior manager. There may also be misunderstandings between the teams or it may be difficult to agree on the prioritisation of elements of an incident. In the worst-case scenario, both teams may blame the other for mistakes and attempt to "score points" for their lack of fault.

The potential for significant reduction in the effectiveness of management of a situation requiring input from both teams means that it is vital that steps are taken to attempt to mediate, and ultimately achieve, effective co-ordination.

Jade Ltd.

For Jade Ltd., the damage to reputation and core operations that could result from an ill-managed crisis should help to motivate staff to endeavour to work together effectively. This being a smaller organization there are fewer places to hide mistakes or work-arounds that the DR or IR team may use. There may be a good reason for their evasion; it may be, for example, that the budget that was allotted to them was insufficient for the process they had hoped to use. However, with such a small organization, especially when the DL and IR teams have to work together, these work-arounds will need to be mutually understood, as well as working for both teams.

The need to have a pre-organised and practiced approach to media queries is essential in this case. Should a significant incident happen on an otherwise slow news day, then any fault in the interaction with the media, which includes control of official social media output, could mean that the event receives greater coverage than expected. This would mean that any absence of clear information could be filled with conjecture. News abhors a vacuum and journalists are well-practiced in the art of filling them – and generally not in favour of those who didn't answer their calls. Ensuring that such queries are answered effectively should be a core part of the creation of disaster and incident response processes for any organization commonly dealing with sensitive information, whether or not that data is involved in the incident.

23

Next Steps for the CIO

'Whut's the plan, Rob?' said one of them.
'Okay, lads, this is what we'll do. As soon as we see somethin',
we'll attack it. Right?'
This caused a cheer.
'Ach, 'tis a good plan,' said Daft Wullie.

Terry Pratchett
Wee Free Men

Introduction

However, where should you go from here?

By this point in the book, you could be in many places. If you have been working along with the book then, by this point, you should have some degree of a functioning incident response organization with some level of documentation, but possibly not yet with specialist training or equipment.

In an ideal world, you would now have the partially trained and somewhat experienced core of an incident response team for your organization.

Or you might have had to throw yourself and your staff at the front of the book and have had to work through your first major security incident.

The luckiest of you will have been reading this entirely theoretically and are wondering how practical any of this will be within your organization, and almost certainly within your budget. You might even be in Rob Anybody's position, and simply have a plan.*

In the years since we initially started considering this book, the threat has changed considerably. We have moved from viruses

---

* Or a "pln" as they often, not being very good with the written word, called them.

and worms and targeted attacks against high-risk organizations through ubiquitous phishing attacks and their derivatives, highly engineered state and organised crime attacks to ransom wear and, by the time you are reading this, almost certainly something new and destructive.

No matter where you are on the resource and experience spectra, it is essential for the survival of almost any business that its ability to continue to operate as an Information Age participant is maintained. A bastion mentality is not practical for all bar a tiny minority of business sectors. Everything from office supplies to payroll to document and file management, by and large, now requires external network connectivity. The next step is to determine how best to assure this, within your organization's risk appetite.

Further Developments

Unless you are really unlucky, your level of incident experience is probably insufficient to have identified any significant and material deficiencies in your planned provision of services and resource. However, it is important not to lose momentum.

In the end, as with so many other aspects of work, it all comes (or should do) down to business risk management. You may be a traditional business with face-to-face operations and strongly consolidated supplier base. You may be a modern business, possibly a startup, with all of your services provided through the cloud. Either model and the many in between have strengths and weaknesses, and it is those weaknesses, at least those critical to supporting ongoing operations, are what you should now focus on. In the absence of real incidents (and of a sufficient variety to test the different aspects of your organization) "what if" scenarios or for the ex-military among you, "table-top exercises" should help you to understand what is critical and what can be managed without and for how long.

First Thoughts

Ensuring that the incident response team has the contacts, and the skill sets to deal with those most critical elements should be a priority. The next most important thing is communications and awareness with the rest of the business and its most critical partners. People must know who to report issues to, and how, and the organizational culture must be such that there is no fear of reporting even if someone has made a contributory error. Things will go wrong and people will make mistakes. Early awareness, and therefore the ability to respond quickly, is almost always more useful than managing to find someone at least partially to blame. In many businesses, one of your most important sets of eyes are your customers, the people who are using your products and services. You may want to have slightly different contact routes through your usual customer support channels, but those teams need to be educated to understand what a security involving incident might look like be aware of what a potential security problem looks like, and empowered to involve your triage team. Many of the attacks, in fact, are customer-facing. Phishing (and its derivatives) and advanced fee frauds, dressed up in your colours, need to be acknowledged, even if just for the awareness and management of potential reputational damage.

The next priority is likely to be technical and resource resilience within the incident response team itself. We have already talked about manning rotas, but we need to consider how this can be maintained in the medium to long term. If you do have active incidents, the work is often very rewarding, and it may be possible to cycle members of other security and IT teams through the incident response organization. This both gives the core members time off rota, providing a chance for training, vacation and other medium duration activities. More importantly, this also will expand the pool of experienced staff you will be able to call on in a crisis, as well as being able to identify possible recruits for permanent incident response positions.

As we move past VOIP to a world of unified communications, the ability to continue to effectively manage incidents, in the event that the main corporate data connectivity is a victim of the situation, is a significant consideration. Maintaining lines of authority and responsibility when your CEO is on the golf course and your CFO is on the beach, is vital if unnecessary delays in approval are not to hamper your activities. Matthew was very lucky that the internet focused worms of 2001 and 2002 had provided security IR with solid executive attention, and the rise of phishing attacks kept it as, albeit to a continuously declining level, an organizational priority. For teams where incidents are rare, minor or internal, ensuring that sufficient focus is maintained will require management effort.

It will be necessary to ensure that back up communications are available, tested, and, in any regulated environment, approved for use with corporate, and potentially customer, sensitive data. Equally, the ability to maintain proper incident records, to the appropriate evidential standard where necessary needs to be considered. Even if this, in the final case, means resorting to pen and paper.

Once you have all the basics in place, and a reasonable outlook for future funding and development, your most appropriate next steps will vary hugely. In a high activity environment, you are likely to be, by the time you have worked through the above, in a situation where you have a skilled and trusted core team and reasonable section of both the business and technical teams, within the organization, that have some experience of working with you in a variety of different contexts. In a low activity organization, you will probably need to focus on maintaining essential skills and the cultural awareness of security response. Unless you are extremely lucky, this is likely to be in the face of business pressures that consider you a burden rather an essential capability. However, in the current environment there are usually regular reminders of major security issues in both the trade, and the mainstream press, that should allow you to retain some degree of executive attention.

Regular exercises, role playing an incident that has happened within your industry sector and involving all aspects of the response organization from technical staff to business executives, may be very useful in keeping the process alive in the absence of actual attacks that need to be dealt with. This is very similar to the requirement to conduct, and participate in regular drills in earthquake zones, and other areas where there is a significant, if irregular, acknowledged risk. Obviously, these exercises need to be infrequent enough that they can gain the appropriate support and attention, particularly from more senior members of the organization.

You may be lucky enough that there is a technical training facility near to you, set up to provide full range immersive incident response and management exercises in the right environment for active, rather than merely "table-top" training.

Industry Good Practice and Benchmarking

Obviously, one of the best ways to know whether or not you are in a "reasonable" or "appropriate" position is to compare yourself against similar organizations.

You may be able to do this through contacts within your industry or local area, through one or more of the International Incident Response Co-Operation organizations or through working with one of the commercial business research organizations.

One of the critical differentiators between what is reasonable for different organizations with regard to incident response is, as we hope to have shown in the case studies, is their size. This usually determines whether you have the ability to work continuously as a 24×7 organization (and therefore need the incident response team to be equivalently available), or whether extended office hours working can be considered normal, with out-of-hours work as the exception when dealing appropriately important or urgent events.

However, as mentioned above, with the increasing use of cloud and other massively virtualised technologies, your ability to actually conduct detailed investigations work will depend on the level of access your technical teams, internal or outsourced, have to the IT systems that provide your infrastructure. Comparison against organizations with similar IT setups, rather than necessarily of the same size or in the same industry sector, may also prove useful.

Digital Forensics

As you gain experience you will find a range of different demands upon your team, and will need, as with any other area of business, to manage conflicting priorities for resources and investment. Because of the nature of financial services, the most significant increase in demand on Matthew's team was for digital forensics services to support counter-fraud and special handling investigations.

As has been discussed previously, the main issue with forensic work, is the length of time it takes. Even in an environment where, despite not being particularly budget restricted, but where staff numbers were a constant executive focus, it was decided by management to maintain this as an internal capability.

Your requirements, drivers and context are likely to vary considerably. Also, the increased ecology of specialist security services, whether "Managed Security Services," "Security As A Service," cloud offerings and niche capabilities means that the decision to provide less regularly required resources, internally or externally, is quite different. Requirements for regular upgrade of specialist technical software and hardware, and the necessity to avoid "skill fade" are going to be essential considerations your decision making.

In general, it is sensible to outsource digital forensics and to engineer your response capabilities to avoid the need to engage such services in the majority of cases.

Incident Confirmation

A crucial and difficult aspect is deciding whether an incident has actually occurred or not. With the rise in legal requirement for mandatory data breach reporting, a lot of focus will need to be on determining whether data has actually been either exposed to or lost to an attacker. As well as having the technical analysis capability, and the necessary level of auditing and monitoring to record and analyse data flows, this will also require extensive and close co-operation with a variety of non-technical teams.

Precisely who these are will depend on your structure, but legal compliance and media are essential suspects. Working with a variety of organizations enabling the executive the executive to understand the business impact on the organization is critical. Many executives have a shallow understanding of the downsides of technology, and surprisingly, an equal lack of understanding of non-core regulatory and legal obligations.

You are likely to find that you quite quickly are forced to become, if not an expert, at least a competent journeymen in many of these areas. As the CIO you are the interface between technical specialists and executive priorities.

Stay Flexible

No matter how the particular threat, and how the organizational requirements change with context, jurisdiction and time, the basic principles or professional incident management should stay the same.

Good organizational awareness and reporting, prompt response, a thorough understanding of the business and its supporting technologies and a dedicated and properly resourced core team should enable you to survive both common and exceptional events. Management flexibility and executive support, as well as a willingness to admit mistakes and modify planned courses of action make it a professional, rather than a technical activity.

Hopefully, you will not gain the battle-hardened experience of multiple days significant incidents, but training the occasional issue and regular review of their people's problems should keep you ready and able to respond when things do go wrong, as they unfortunately will.

Just remember the words of the sage: "Don't Panic."

Index

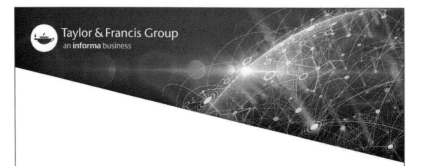

Taylor & Francis Group
an **informa** business

Taylor & Francis eBooks

www.taylorfrancis.com

A single destination for eBooks from Taylor & Francis
with increased functionality and an improved user
experience to meet the needs of our customers.

90,000+ eBooks of award-winning academic content in
Humanities, Social Science, Science, Technology, Engineering,
and Medical written by a global network of editors and authors.

TAYLOR & FRANCIS EBOOKS OFFERS:

A streamlined
experience for
our library
customers

A single point
of discovery
for all of our
eBook content

Improved
search and
discovery of
content at both
book and
chapter level

REQUEST A FREE TRIAL
support@taylorfrancis.com

 Routledge
Taylor & Francis Group

 CRC Press
Taylor & Francis Group

Printed and bound by CPI Group (UK) Ltd, Croydon, CR0 4YY

23/10/2024

01777671-0010